06/2020

THE SEARCH FOR MEANING
IN THE WORKPLACE

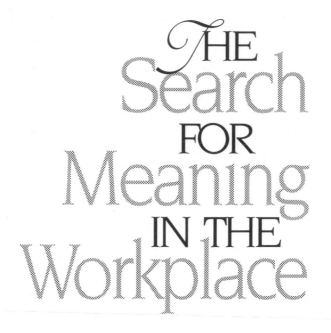

The Search FOR Meaning IN THE Workplace

Thomas H. Naylor,
William H. Willimon,
& Rolf Österberg

Abingdon Press
Nashville

THE SEARCH FOR MEANING IN THE WORKPLACE

Library of Congress Cataloging-in-Publication Data

Naylor, Thomas H., 1936–
    The search for meaning in the workplace / Thomas H. Naylor, William H. Willimon, and Rolf Österberg.
        p.   cm.
    Includes bibliographical references.
    ISBN 0-687-01548-0 (pbk. : alk. paper)
    1. Work ethic. 2. Work—Philosophy. 3. Work—Psychology.
    4. Meaning (Philosophy) I. Österberg, Rolf. II. Willimon, William H.
    III. Title.
    HD4905.N39 1996
    158.7—dc20   96-21841
                                                                                    CIP

96 97 98 99 00 01 02 03 04 05—10 9 8 7 6 5 4 3 2 1

MANUFACTURED IN THE UNITED STATES OF AMERICA

Contents

Soul-Searching

In *The Search for Meaning,* cowritten by two of us, Thomas and Will, we put forth the proposition that the search for meaning involves coming to grips with what it is to be a human being who lives, loves, works, plays, suffers, and dies. Our search is a search for grounding—a sense of connectedness to ourselves, to others, to history, to nature, and to the ground of our being. A strong sense

---

Soul Crafting

$\mathcal{T}$he bottom line of the search for meaning is soul crafting—the care and nurturing of our soul, possibly our only salvage from death's oblivion. Our soul is the sum of our deeds, our work, our creations, our experience, our love, our joy, our pain, and our suffering. Throughout our entire life, our soul is continuously in the process of becoming.

THOMAS H. NAYLOR
WILLIAM H. WILLIMON
MAGDALENA R. NAYLOR
The Search for Meaning [1]

---

of meaning is what motivates us to get out of bed each morning and confront yet another day of life and all its uncertainty, to transform our fate into our destiny, to make life more an adventure than a bore.[2]

For some artists, writers, musicians, physicians, and clergy, the meaning of life lies entirely in their work—in their creations, in their patients, and in their congregations. Many corporate executives, politicians, and government officials seek meaning through manipulation, power, and control. Still others work only because it enables them to accumulate vast wealth and material possessions. But for millions of people, work is a necessary evil engaged in primarily to support themselves and their families. For them, work is not a source of pleasure but rather a boring, repetitive, and unchallenging way of making a living. The people who enjoy their work and find it truly meaningful are a minority of the population.

In the final chapter of *The Search for Meaning*, we concluded that "the purpose of life is to die happy." But how can one die happy, if one's work has no meaning? Is it possible to find meaningful work? If so, how? That is the subject of this book.

In collaboration with Rolf Österberg, the author of *Corporate Renaissance*, we have expanded the chapter "The Search for Meaning in the Workplace" in our previous book into this extended, in-depth study.

The Meaning of Work

The business life of the whole world is on its way to a deep crisis—an existential crisis over the purpose and meaning of work and business.

ROLF ÖSTERBERG
Corporate Renaissance [3]

Since this collaborative effort is both a special case and a logical extension of *The Search for Meaning*, the chapters on the life matrix, community in the workplace, and management philosophy closely parallel their counterparts in the original book. Where appropriate, throughout this book, we shall draw on our previous works, *The Search for Meaning* and *Corporate Renaissance.*

Thomas H. Naylor
William H. Willimon
Rolf Österberg

THE SEARCH FOR MEANING
IN THE WORKPLACE

Morfar, Lucas, Max, and the Playhouse

————*Chapter 1*————

THE SEARCH FOR MEANING

Creating meaning may be the most important managerial task of the future.

Companies must find ways to harness soul-searching on the job, not just gloss over or merely avoid it.

MARTHA NICHOLS
HARVARD BUSINESS REVIEW

The Playhouse

The summer of 1994 in Sweden was very hot—the hottest and driest July since record-keeping began in 1756. One of us, Rolf, spends each summer at his vacation house on Vätö Island just off the coast of Sweden on the Baltic Sea. He and his wife, Carol, had planned a glorious summer of swimming, boating, and resting in the shaded hammocks. And that is what they did with the exception of one unexpected event: The Playhouse.

Early in the summer Lucas, who was four and a half, and Max, who was a little over three, reminded their *morfar* (Swedish for grandfather) that the previous fall he had suggested that the three of them build a playhouse. After talking it over, they jointly decided to go ahead with the project. The *work* began.

Several important decisions had to be made by the fearless threesome. First, they had to decide where to locate the house. Long—and sometimes intense—negotiations followed. Max wanted it to be easily accessible from his room in the big house and proposed a location adjacent the entry stairs. Morfar didn't think that was such a good idea. Lucas wanted to give special recognition to the fact that the playhouse was to be "our house" and suggested a spot far away from the big house, "maybe behind the barn or someplace like that." Morfar, more concerned about heat exhaustion than location, tried to direct the boys' attention toward a shady spot. The pros and cons of each possible location were carefully evaluated. Finally they came to the unanimous decision to erect the playhouse near a side wall of the big house. Max liked this alternative because the playhouse would be close to his room, Lucas because it would be clearly separated from the main house, and Morfar because the location was shaded for at least a few hours each day.

Their next step was to figure out the size and the height of the playhouse. Morfar brought out folding rulers and other devices in order to measure the exact dimensions. Lucas and Max were not very enthusiastic about this idea and opted for a less precise and less complex approach. They gathered old planks from the woodpile behind the barn. They then laid them out, made marks with crayons, and stood inside the marks in order to get a feel for and determine if that was the size playhouse they wanted.

Then the real construction began. For an hour or two each day, they worked together. They selected planks together. They carried planks together. They sawed planks together. They chose which planks to use where together. They chose the nails together. They hammered together. They had a great time being together, and they grew closer with each working session. They put much love into their work, and they all longed for the next working session. Each night after telling Morfar and Mormor (Swedish for grandmother) "night-night," they added a special "good night" for the playhouse, telling it, "How much we hope you will grow tomorrow."

Fun at Work

There's no reason that work has to be suffused with seriousness. Professionalism can be worn lightly. Fun is a stimulant to people. They enjoy their work more and work more productively.

HERB KELLEHER, CEO
Southwest Airlines

By early fall the project was nearing completion. The walls were standing, and the roof was on. All that remained was installation of a door. Earlier the three had decided to delay the flooring and the painting until the following summer. After some discussion, Lucas and Max made it clear that the door must have a real keyhole, a working lock, and a key. "Morfar," said Lucas, "you must understand that we need to be able to lock the house." They found just the door they needed in one of the sheds, used the saw to fit it to the size of the frame, attached the hinges, and mounted it in place.

Conviviality

*T*he autonomous and creative intercourse among persons, and the intercourse of persons with the environment; and this in contrast with the conditioned response of persons to the demands made upon them by others, and by a man-made environment. I consider conviviality to be individual freedom realized in personal interdependence and, as such, an intrinsic ethical value. I believe that, in any society, as conviviality is reduced below a certain level, no amount of industrial productivity can effectively satisfy the needs it creates among society's members.

IVAN ILLICH
Tools for Conviviality[1]

Then came an unforgettable moment. Lucas, followed by Max, looked at Morfar with the most shining face he had ever seen. Practically bursting out of his body, Lucas said, "Morfar, we did it—we built the house together." At that moment, the joy, the happiness, the pride, the love they shared became very tangible. They hugged, they kissed, and they celebrated by putting two wooden flags on the roof, one painted in the blue and yellow Swedish colors, the other in red, white, and blue to honor Carol, who is an American.

Then an unexpected moment of sadness came over the three of them. They all felt it, but some time passed before one of them, little Max, expressed it: "Morfar, what shall we do next?" Only then did the significance of their summer adventure become clear: They had inadvertently stumbled upon an almost perfect example of

Convivial Work

A post-industrial society must and can be so con-
structed that no one person's ability to express him- or
herself in work will require as a condition the enforced
labor or the enforced learning or the enforced consumption of another.

IVAN ILLICH
Tools for Conviviality[2]

meaningful work. Max's poignant words had driven the point home
with amazing clarity. Yes, they felt good about having completed
the project. It was also a nice feeling to discover that they could
actually build a playhouse. But, what was next? What should they
do, now that the playhouse was complete?

Work on the playhouse was meaningful to all three—Lucas,
Max, and Morfar. In cooperation they had created new insights
about themselves as individuals and as a *team.* Probably the most
exciting insight to Lucas and Max was that they could actually work
together with their morfar. As they expressed it, "Together we
could make a playhouse." As for Morfar, his most important insights were about patience and cooperation. In cooperation they
had found that they were more than three individuals playing out
their usual roles. Without giving it much thought, the three of them
had grown spiritually, intellectually, and emotionally, and they had
enjoyed themselves as well. Life and work were seamlessly joined;
they were heartened, energized, and immediately started to look
for other projects—for more work.

Together Max, Lucas, and Morfar had decided what work was
to be done, how to do it, who would do what, and when it was to be
done. They had discovered that the process of building the playhouse was at least as meaningful as the product itself.

At the end of the summer, Morfar reflected, "I probably don't
need to tell you how much I'm looking forward to next summer's
work on the playhouse with my grandsons. (There are four of them
now!) Our time together will be meaningful; we will be close, and
we will grow. There will be no distances between us and no secrets.

And no one of us will be more important or valuable than any other."

What determines whether or not one's work is meaningful? Does it depend entirely on the job itself? Are some jobs inherently more meaningful than others? What role does the employer play in influencing the meaningfulness of a particular job? What about the attitude of the employee? How does one go about finding meaningful work?

Before turning to the answers to these questions and others, we shall each share the story of our own searches for meaning in the workplace beginning with Rolf and followed by Will and Thomas.

A Businessman's Odyssey

I spent the years between 1959 and 1984 in Swedish business. For twenty-three of these years, I held different CEO positions in organizations and corporations mainly in the media industry. I also served as a member of the board of directors of some twenty-five different trade associations and companies (apart from media, in industries as diverse as manufacturing, electronics, real estate, hotels, and finance). I left business in November of 1984. I did so after a long struggle within myself about the meaning of what I was doing, about the meaning of work, of business, and after severely questioning the relation between people and business. Since then, I have spent my life thinking, writing, and lecturing about the larger meaning of work and business as human enterprises.

This is the road I traveled to get where I am now. I'm not submitting it to you because I think I'm such an interesting or unique person. I'm submitting it because I know that there are many others going through similar processes and, from my own experience, I know how important it is not to feel alone.

I was born in 1933 and grew up in Stockholm, Sweden, in a conservative upper-middle-class family. There was no business tradition in our family, and becoming a businessman was not any part of my thoughts about the future. In fact, as was the case with most youngsters of my generation, I never really sat down to ponder what I wanted to do with my life. Rather I tried to get a feel for the thoughts and dreams surrounding me in my world—above all, those of my parents—about my uncertain future. "What do they expect of me?" was the question dwelling within me, rather than: "What do I really want to do?"

Initially I considered only two options—either follow in the footsteps of my father or those of my Austrian grandfather. My father was a mathematical genius and a highly respected professor at the Swedish Royal Institute of Technology. My maternal grandfather had been a diplomat. Rather early on, I came to the conclusion that mathematics or anything close to it was out of the question; it did not take many school years to discover that I (in what was probably a form of rebellion against my father) simply disliked mathematics. Therefore, I, at the age of fourteen or fifteen, decided on a career in the diplomatic corps. I knew that two things were required—languages and a law degree. In our equivalent of high school, I concentrated on languages. Each summer I spent half my vacation working and the other half traveling—often hitchhiking abroad. I traveled to Switzerland, Germany, France, and England primarily to improve my foreign language skills.

Having finished high school and completed my military service, I decided to take a year off before entering law school. Using a government premium I had earned during my military service, I went to Spain to learn Spanish. I had sufficient funds to study for five months at the University of Barcelona; then I took a job as a hotel interpreter, which enabled me to stay another five months. Fluent in four foreign languages, I returned to Sweden and entered law school.

While still in law school, I married and gave up my plans for a diplomatic career. Discussing our future together, my wife and I concluded that diplomatic life—moving from one country to another—wouldn't suit us. We wanted children and wanted them to be rooted in Sweden. So there I was, having no idea of what to do with my law degree. I decided to "wait and see" and accepted an internship for a couple of years as an assistant judge in one of the local Stockholm courts. During the internship, I got my first job offer—as legal secretary to the Swedish Confederation of Employers. I was told that this was a "position with very good prospects," accepted the offer, and started practicing law. I came to like it and had a good time. Above all, I liked the trials. I liked presenting the cases, bringing the evidence, examining the witnesses, and presenting the summations. I often felt that I was playing one of the main parts in a play, and it was a very special feeling when I was able to convince the audience—the judges—that my case was airtight! "Maybe, this, after all, is my line?" I began thinking.

However, it did not last more than a couple of years. I happened to handle some cases for newspapers, and I was offered and accepted the position as president and CEO of the Swedish Newspapers Association. As this was a prestigious position—the Press was then still considered to be "the fourth estate"—the fact that such a young person was elected to this post attracted a lot of media attention, and I started feeling the "sweets" of power and position—of being important—and now, for the first time, the idea of making business a career came into my head.

One of my primary tasks with the Association was to conduct labor negotiations for the industry. However, the fact that I spent much of my time negotiating work and working conditions did not cause me to ponder more deeply the meaning of work other than as the production of goods and services in exchange for paychecks. I was still rather conservative. Production—and profitable production—was, as I saw it, the very driving force for progress, and progress was tantamount to economic growth. Economic growth in turn came about as a result of the interplay between labor and capital. The fruits of this interplay should be distributed in a "fair" way—even though fairness was always tilted toward the managers and investors, since, without risk capital, the economy could not grow. And that was the whole idea, wasn't it?

My doubts and questions regarding work came later. There was, however, another issue that did catch my interest during these years—the issue of *intuition*. During my early years as a labor negotiator, I put much effort into painstakingly planning each negotiating round. I made plans and worked out strategies and saw my work as virtually a game of chess. After some time, though, I realized that these plans and strategies were not only boring, but they rarely worked out (they were easily upset by unexpected moves by the other party). They also blinded me and prevented me from hearing what the other parties were really saying. Slowly, I started *feeling* my way through the negotiation rounds rather than using my head and eventually dropped all planning and went into negotiations without any preparation at all, trusting that my intuition would lead to improved outcomes. And it did.

I stayed with the Association for nearly seven years. I liked my job—which in addition to labor negotiations, mainly consisted of lobbying for the industry's interests. But then I began to feel that it was time to move on. When I was offered the position of executive vice president and deputy CEO of the Dagens Nyheter Group—Scandinavia's largest newspaper company, employing some 4,500 persons—I did not hesitate in accepting the offer. At the same time, the chairman of the Association's board decided to resign and I was elected to succeed him, which meant that I continued to be involved in the newspaper industry's labor relations. It was at this point that things began to change for me.

For the first time I actually met some of the people whose working conditions I had been involved in negotiating. I came close to them, saw them pursuing their work, came to appreciate their skills, and became friends with many of them. They were no longer mere negotiating units but human beings with the same kinds of problems, the same kinds of dreams as mine. At that time, my marriage started to deteriorate; my wife (obviously fed up with my working hours) wanted a divorce to start a new life with another man. The divorce resulted in the collapse of the very foundation of my life, my family (we had three children). This was a real blow to me—the most traumatic event in my life. Looking at myself and at the people around me, I, for the first time, started asking myself, "Why am I doing this? What does this all mean? Is it really right?" However, I managed to put aside these troubling questions—at least a little longer. After all, as a business executive, I wasn't supposed to contemplate the meaning of life; my role was to run the company. And to boost my own feeling of self-importance, I would add, "I am responsible to the shareholders and to my fellow employees." Although I did begin spending more time with my children—and we have indeed become quite close—I continued to take on more and more work, further numbing my growing feelings of self-doubt.

My denial strategy worked for several more years, but by the end of the 1970s it was beginning to wear thin. My feelings of dissatis-faction, emptiness, and meaninglessness became stronger and stronger. As I have described in more detail in *Corporate Renaissance,* these feelings became more intense during labor negotiations. The final rounds of these negotiations usually took place at night. As the leader of the negotiating team, I often had to spend several hours alone during these marathon evening sessions. While the union leaders were discussing management's "last bid" with their committee, and my committee was trying to get some sleep, in order to stay awake I would walk around the nearby neighborhood. Tired and exhausted, I found that my usual "protective shield" would begin to fail. My feelings of dissatisfaction and emptiness kept rising to the surface; my questions of meaning would not go away.

During these lonely night hours, it became increasingly clear to me that management viewed labor merely as a commodity to be purchased at the lowest possible price and used as a tool for achieving the goals and objectives we had for the companies we were running. But it didn't stop there. In observing and talking with union representatives, it became obvious that they too had a similar view of the world. They were there to sell their members— their time, skills, and part of their lives—for as high a price as possible, and the individual workers viewed the companies where they worked as their tools—tools to achieve their personal, finan-cial, and career objectives. Before long I started to realize that I too was using my company as a tool—a tool to increase my income, to enhance my career, and to enable me to reach the position of power I felt I so richly deserved. And, of course, I was a tool as well—a tool of the members of the boards of directors of the organizations in which I was either an employee or a board member myself. My existentialist questions about life and the meaning of my work began to increase exponentially.

"I don't want to be just a tool!" I said to myself. "I'm sure my coworkers don't want to be tools, either. Why do we do this to ourselves? What has made us accept these mechanistic, almost machinelike relations between people and business? There must be another way of looking at work and business than this. It's inhuman. Is there no other driving force than money? Is 'Economic Growth' the only solution to the problems of our society? Although we have achieved one of the highest standards of living in the world, why are we not happy, harmonious, at peace with ourselves? Aren't the high number of job-stress-related diseases and deaths a sign that something is wrong? The increasing drug and alcohol abuse? And the high suicide rate among young people? And why all this fear? Fear at our workplaces? Fear in our societal lives? Why are our political campaigns ("vote with us, or risk losing this or that") based so often on fear? Why are so many people separated? Why are there so many special interest groups? Why is it always 'us' versus 'them'?"

Then I became afraid. "What will happen to me, my position, my future, my finances, if I think along these lines," I began saying to myself. "I need to be careful not to think myself 'out of the market.'" I began to work even harder to try to suppress all these questions, doubts, and emotions. In addition to overworking, I started indulging in travel and alcohol. Of course, none of this helped and I decided to pursue the final rescue—to change jobs. I was offered what many considered to be the ideal "dream job"— President and CEO of Sweden's largest film company, AB Svensk Filmindustri, the company that produced many of the Ingmar Bergman films. "To work with film—art—must be different," was my wishful thinking. It did not, of course, take long to realize that the film business is no different from any other business. The "old" questions and doubts soon returned. In addition, the company, somewhat to my surprise, was in rather bad financial shape, and I had to work very hard (which probably kept me there) to get it back on its feet. Once I had accomplished this four years later, the company was sold, and I resigned and took on a short-term assignment as the chairman of a magazine publishing company. Finally, one day at the end of November 1984, it became clear that I had to leave the business world. "This is killing you," I heard my inner voice say. "You must get out, free yourself, and gain some insight about what is going on within you. Not least, you need to put your life in perspective." I immediately sent out letters of resignation from all my business-related activities, and my life as a businessman came to an end.

Having resigned from all these businesses, I discovered two things. First, when I began expressing my doubts and questions, I discovered that I was not alone. From many directions and from people in all layers of society came the same signals of dissatisfaction, the same doubts about the meaningfulness of our way of looking at work and business, the same doubts about the economy as the only driving force. Second, much to my chagrin, I discovered that I no longer had an identity of my own. I had so identified myself—and been identified by others—with my professional roles that I had lost myself. I found myself walking in a quagmire without any firm ground under my feet. I started a long—still continuing—strenuous, but increasingly joyful, journey back to my true self. It was inevitable that my quest for meaning would become an integral part of this journey—a fascinating, sometimes difficult, arduous walk along a spiritual path.

In the fall of 1986, this path led me to a conference at Findhorn, a spiritual center in Northern Scotland. A few days before leaving Sweden, I had a hunch that I should go there instead of to a conference in London, which I had originally planned to attend. I flew to Aberdeen and took the train to the small town of Forres. On the train ride something happened: I had a premonition that, at the conference, I would meet the real love of my life. The feeling was so strong that once I arrived in Findhorn, I started carefully observing the female participants. "Could that be she? No, probably not. But maybe that one? No, I don't think so." And so it went in my head. It was a very weird feeling. Then there she was, a Ph.D. in psychology from California—standing in a small group of people involved in discussion. I joined the group. We began talking, finding out that our ways of looking at things, our interests, our thoughts, our emotions, and even our experiences coincided in a remarkable way. The following afternoon, she confused me by asking whether I felt like "playing hooky." I was not familiar with the word "hooky" and thought she meant "hockey." Since I could not imagine an ice hockey rink in that little town and had never practiced land hockey, I rather brusquely responded, "No, but I would love to have a walk." And walk we did. Four days later we had decided to share the rest of our lives together. Without thinking (if we had, we probably would have found too many obstacles), we decided to share our time between our two countries.

We walk together. It's not an easy walk. Now and then, there are big boulders on our path. Now and then, we meet storms and thunder. There is also much sunshine, and the sun shines brighter when we have overcome some obstacles on our way and feel that we have taken yet another step in our evolution, our human evolution. Yes, we do work together, also in our professional roles. Actually, much of my work would not have come about without Carol's insightful input, and she often tells me how much my input means to her work—devising theories and practical methods for removing and changing what appear to be the very stumbling blocks of human progress: our core beliefs (so often hidden in our subconscious). We live in harmony between ourselves. We live in harmony with our families (between us we have seven children and ten grandchildren), and we live in harmony with the natural environment surrounding us in our two countries. We have fun. And, we have friends, not the "social" friends and business acquaintances I used to spend so much time with, but real friends. For the first time, I lead a rich life, though not with the affluence to which I was once accustomed. I am doing exactly what I want to do and when I want to do it. I write and travel around the world speaking about meaning and, by doing that, I learn more and more and find more and more meaning. Never have I enjoyed work as I do now.

A Pastor's Pilgrimage

I was raised in a family which embodied the fabled Protestant work ethic. My mother took great delight in her ability to perform hard work. She passed on to her children much faith in the power of hard work to overcome most obstacles in life. She possessed a firm conviction, a conviction I have come to question in later life, that there was absolutely no problem in life that could not be solved simply by working hard.

In my youth, I had the usual round of after-school jobs—life guard, camp counselor, janitor, salesclerk—which initiated me into the world of work. My most memorable youthful work experience extended for three summers just before and during my first years of college, when I worked in a factory in my hometown. There I experienced an initial joy at doing "grown-up work," working on an assembly line, using machines, producing things. However, that initial joy quickly faded as I settled into a job that was repetitive, boring, and uninteresting. As one of my college classmates working alongside me said, "You can learn the skills required for this job in about three weeks and there are guys who have been doing them here for thirty years!"

Only males worked in our part of the factory, and most of them spent the entire day from the moment the whistle blew in the morning until the time the whistle blew in the late afternoon bragging about their sexual exploits, killing time, and relieving boredom by poking fun at one another. Most of my coworkers were African Americans. This was the early sixties when racial integration was inching its way into the American South. On the assembly line, I saw the effects of racism firsthand. One of my great surprises was to discover how "unbusiness-like" business really was in regard to racial mores. That is, none of the black workers was ever promoted to a managerial position on the assembly line, even a low-level managerial position. All of the assembly-line workers were black; all of their supervisors were white. The system seemed so irrational because many of the black workers were obviously more intelligent, more highly motivated, and better informed than their white supervisors. Again and again, in summers at that factory, I would watch as inept white workers were promoted over their black counterparts, simply because they were white. This seemed not only unjust, but bad for business.

No doubt in reaction to this irrational system, many of the black workers eventually stopped trying and through various passive-aggressive means took out their frustration and anger at the company through shoddy workmanship and goofing off whenever the supervisor's back was turned.

The man who ran this company, the person who had given me my job, was a born-again, evangelical Christian.

My job in the factory had one powerful effect on me. Summers working there were strong incentive to do well in college! One of my great goals in college was to make grades good enough to ensure that I would never need to work on an assembly line for the rest of my life. Yet I am still haunted by memories of those summers' experience, thinking from time to time about the people who worked there with me when I was a teenager, who are working there yet.

After college, I went to seminary, having a growing sense that I was being called by God and the church to the pastoral ministry. Looking back, I realize that one attraction of the Christian ministry was that I was entering a profession where I did not have to work. That admission comes as a surprise to me now. Although a pastor's life has a certain amount of routine, drudgery, and repetitiveness, it is far more eventful and challenging than life on an assembly line. A pastor has a significant amount of control over his or her day. There is much variety and emotional and intellectual challenge.

Pastors have a fair amount of "discretionary time." As one of my parishioners put it to me, "You preachers are privileged—you can read a book anytime you want to." I very much enjoy the intellectual opportunities of life as a pastor. We are privileged in having time to read, pray, and reflect, time that many others do not have. Along with this privilege comes for me a sense of responsibility. Since I have been given so much discretionary time, free space in order to read and to reflect, I ought to use it well. Once when one of my friends commented to me about how much work I do, how many books and articles I write, and so forth, I told him, "Perhaps I do this out of a sense of guilt. That is, I realize that I have never worked a day of my life as hard as my mother worked on most days of her life." My mother was a high school teacher who in the summers ran, as part of her work as a home economist, a cannery for home gardeners. I felt privileged not to have to work that hard—and also obliged. The springs of commitment for our work run deep. Funny, how we bring to our work some of our deepest memories, most secret and powerful needs.

On the other hand, I quickly learned as a pastor some of the difficulties of pastoral work. For one thing, one must work as a pastor for a couple of hundred bosses. In a sense everybody in the congregation is your boss—each with a clearly defined sense of what you ought to do. Additionally, pastoral work is so often ill-defined and open-ended that a pastor's work is never done. Pastors are some of the hardest working people I have ever known—and the laziest. A pastor has dozens of bosses in the congregation and yet, in a sense, no boss. Pastors are probably the least supervised and accountable of professionals—unless it is the profession of being a professor! This means that pastors must define who they are, what their jobs really consist of, and how they ought to use their time. Pastors who fail to take charge of their schedule and their commitments are usually yanked to and fro by dozens of "necessary" obligations. As Henri Nouwen puts it, "If pastors don't know the absolutely essential thing to do, they do the merely important." Because so much of what a pastor does is important, pastors can drown in running to and fro from various important, but not necessarily essential, activities.[3]

Eventually I left the pastoral ministry when I was invited to become a professor at a seminary. I now work as a campus minister and professor at the university. Being a professor has some of the work characteristics of being a pastor. A professor has a large amount of discretionary time, has privileged time to write, to read, to reflect. Again, this open-ended, self-defined quality leads professors, like pastors, to be either extremely driven and hard-working or very lazy.

As a professor I have intensely enjoyed the task of teaching—being exposed to bright, young, developing minds.

I have also enjoyed writing, writing an embarrassingly large number of books and articles. I wonder why I do this. What are the deep-seated, undefined and subtle, but nevertheless very powerful needs that I am meeting through such a large amount of writing? Why do I work?

As a campus minister, I work with young people who are preparing to go to work. Many of them are deeply fearful that what happened to their parents in work will happen to them.

"My old man busted his butt off for GM, then at fifty, they laid him off. So what's the use?" was how one student put it.

"I'm frightened that what happened to my law professor will happen to me when I'm a lawyer," said another.

As a pastor, I also listen to those who work. I've noted in listening some common themes:

1. Most of us spend most of our time, particularly our time interacting with others, at work. Therefore, the work environment is a large determinant of our emotional and spiritual well-being.
2. Many people love their work, but rarely for the money. For many, work is a challenge to be met, a game to be played, a possibility to be fulfilled.
3. Because much of our own work requires much interaction with other persons, people with few "people skills" have a miserable time at work.
4. Much modern work is repetitive, boring, and dull; therefore, for many, work is a mere means to an end. They work only to get away from work and engage in their hobby, leisure activities, or family life where their real gifts are exercised.

The themes my listening uncovers suggest that we are in a crisis of work. The old "Protestant work ethic" has been thrown into question. That ethic under which I was raised is dissipating. Work is being emptied of some of its sacred status. Few look upon their job as vocation, a call from God. Are the sacrifices we make for our job worth the cost? Is there any long-term or longer good being realized by the expenditure of our lives at work?

Recently, I spent extended time with a group of friends from college, talking about what we had learned about life since college. Every one of them expressed envy of me in my work situation. Unlike them, in their jobs in real estate sales, law, or merchandising, I had a sense of being part of some larger good. I had the opportunity to do good for people. I had discretionary time to read and to think. A couple even admitted that they wished they had the courage to go back to school and become a minister or a professor. They thus reminded me of the blessedness of my job, which I experience as a vocation.

An Economist's Quest

My search for meaning in the workplace began with a curbside soft-drink stand and a neighborhood newspaper delivery route followed by mindless backbreaking high school and college summer jobs with the Mississippi Highway Department and the Sun Oil Company. From the crusty rednecks with whom I worked in the Highway Department, I discovered that not everyone in the 1950s in Mississippi had been to college—or even high school for that matter—and that even the poorest whites needed someone to look down upon, in this case poor, uneducated blacks. During the summers of 1955 to 1957, I earned almost enough money cutting trails through the snake-infested swamps of Mississippi and Louisiana with a machete to pay my way to engineering school at Columbia University. Neither the intense summer heat, humidity, yellow jackets, nor cottonmouth moccasins are forgotten. Being surrounded by five angry cottonmouths in an area so thick you couldn't swing your brush hook to protect yourself makes engineering school look like a bed of roses.

Throughout high school and during my first three years of college before entering Columbia, I had always wanted to be an electrical engineer. There was only one catch. Having been strongly influenced by my girlfriend's father, who was himself an electrical engineer, I had absolutely no idea what electrical engineers did. Indeed, in Jackson, Mississippi, where I had grown up in the 1950s, there were no electrical engineers.

During the summer of 1957 prior to entering Columbia, I was required to attend a five-week engineering camp in Bantam, Connecticut. Each week we would visit large manufacturing plants in the area to see what real-live electrical engineers did at IBM, General Electric, and Consolidated Edison. In several of these plants there were two or three hundred engineers seated at drafting tables in one huge room with no windows. Five plant visits convinced me that electrical engineering was definitely not for me, and I switched over to industrial engineering, which was less technical and more business-oriented. However, by the time I graduated from Columbia I was beginning to have real doubts about whether I even liked machines.

Summer jobs at International Paper Company (IPCO) after each year at Columbia gave me my first exposure to Corporate America. The first summer I worked on a project aimed at installing a sophisticated computer-based modeling system at five paper mills in the South. I got to do a lot of traveling working in the different mills and the pay was quite good. It was also my first exposure to the divisive nature of corporate politics and to executive burnout. On balance I was attracted by the money and glamour of a large company and the opportunity to apply some of my newly acquired analytical skills.

My second summer at IPCO was an unmitigated disaster. I was assigned to a sixty-year-old alcoholic whose tenure at IPCO was assured only because he was the fishing buddy of the division general manager. There was no plan for my summer stay and I had virtually nothing to do. To overcome the boredom, I spent endless hours playing bridge and pinochle with my colleagues who also had little to do. On one occasion my boss wrecked the car of my office mate en route from the local gin mill at three o'clock in the afternoon. Whenever I hear stories comparing indolent government bureaucrats with highly motivated managers in the competitive, efficient private sector, I always think of IPCO.

Although the IPCO experience had raised many questions in my mind about whether life in Corporate America was all that it was cracked up to be, I was already committed to entering Indiana University's MBA program to specialize in the use of computers in solving managerial decision-making problems. Getting in on the ground floor of computers and learning to program an IBM 650 were very exciting. Otherwise, business school was boring and unchallenging. Endless corporate war stories told by I.U.'s faculty cast further doubt in my mind about a career in business. A not-particularly-interesting summer job in the sterile bureaucratic world of Dow Chemical Company pushed me over the brink. It was clear that I could never be happy working for a large corporation.

During my last semester at I.U., I became interested in economics—particularly mathematical economics—and decided to pursue a Ph.D. at Tulane University. This enabled me to combine my three loves: mathematics, economics, and computers. To finance my Ph.D., I introduced quantitative courses to Tulane business undergraduates. It was very satisfying to be on the cutting edge of undergraduate business education.

So brisk was the demand for economists trained in mathematics and computers when I completed my Ph.D. in 1964 that I received thirteen academic job offers. Duke University's offer—the lowest salary of the lot—was the one I accepted. Since half my salary at Duke was paid by a National Science Foundation grant, the first thing I did was negotiate my freedom from being told on what to do research. Although I enjoyed teaching, it was abundantly clear that the name of the game at Duke was publications and research grants. Playing the game enabled me to be promoted to full professor two and one-half years after I was hired as an assistant professor.

Even though I taught at Duke thirty years, teaching never again provided me the emotional high I experienced before I became a full professor. The meaning in my life came mostly from activities outside the academy—electoral politics, consulting, starting my own business, trips to the Soviet Union, and publishing articles in the *New York Times*. Even though I enjoyed an incredible amount of freedom at Duke, I resented virtually all of the authority figures—department chairpersons, deans, and university presidents. I never liked being told what to do. Power struggles with deans and department chairpersons were the rule.

In 1971 I started my own political consulting firm, which evolved into a multimillion-dollar computer software business with more than fifty employees before it was sold to a group of German investors in 1980. My motives in starting Social Systems, Inc. (SSI) were threefold. First, I was looking for something to allay the boredom of the academy. Second, I had an intense desire to do my own thing. Third, I enjoyed the power and prestige of hobnobbing with the CEOs of Fortune 500 companies.

Shortly after we began successfully marketing our $70,000 computer software system known as SIMPLAN to companies such as General Motors, United Airlines, Monsanto, and Texaco, the novelty of running my own business began to wear thin. In all too many cases, it was I who had to fly to places like Akron, Ohio, to close a sale. To pay the bills we had to sell a couple of SIMPLAN installations each month—a source of considerable anxiety and stress. So great was the financial pressure to make sales, that we often resorted to strong high-pressure tactics to persuade multibillion-dollar companies to commit to our product. Reflecting on those hectic years of my life is a source of pain and embarrassment. Since I had co-signed the loans used to finance the development of SIMPLAN, until the company became profitable in 1978, the only escape path open to me would have involved personal bankruptcy. And all of this took its toll on my family, resulting in divorce.

Undercapitalization, the failure to hire a first-rate marketing professional, and my own heavy-handed management style all contributed to my feeling that I was more of a slave to the employees than their boss. Perhaps the happiest day of my life was when the company was sold for a modest profit in 1980—free at last! By sheer luck we avoided having to deal with competing software products on microcomputers, which appeared three years later selling for only $300. I can hardly imagine what it would have been like to adapt to such a competitive shock!

Returning to full-time teaching and research in the early 1980s brought me little joy. Cranking out more technical books and articles had little meaning for me. It took me almost four years to recover emotionally from the loss of my recalcitrant problem child SSI—the greatest adventure in my life up to that time. Only by getting heavily involved with the Soviet Union and Eastern Europe as a self-appointed, unpaid cheerleader for Mikhail S. Gorbachev was I able to cope with my angst and boredom with academic life. However, there was one bright light at the end of my career at Duke—teaching undergraduates. During the late 1980s, I began offering a series of popular freshman seminars, including "The

Search for Meaning." I found first-year students at Duke to be bright-eyed and bushy-tailed—a source of considerable joy as well as intellectual stimulation. But even undergraduate teaching had its dark side.

So intense is the pressure for grades these days at places like Duke and Middlebury College that one must be prepared to do battle with students, their parents, and various academic administrators whenever one gives a grade below a B. To give a student a D or an F is tantamount to committing an unforgivable sin for which one is held accountable.

Even with as much freedom as one enjoys at the university, there are still moral and ethical issues to be confronted. Most universities such as Duke still have ROTC programs, which offer their participants full scholarships for four years and a military commission upon graduation. ROTC programs are an important source of financial support. But the aim of ROTC is to train young American men and women to be efficient killers. Paradoxically, while American medical schools are teaching physicians how to save lives, professors of military science at these same institutions are helping produce more trained killers. Since my office was right across the hall from an ROTC classroom, I was reminded of this troubling paradox daily. Regrettably, I never managed to muster the courage to challenge ROTC at Duke.

Thus after thirty years of marching to the beat of the Duke University drum, I took early retirement at the end of 1993 and moved to Charlotte, Vermont, where I read, think, and write. I am accountable only to myself, my family, my community, and my Creator. For the first time since I closed my neighborhood soft-drink business in the 1940s, I am truly doing my own thing. But unlike the past, I now devote much more time and energy to what has become the most important challenge of my life—integration of the professional, spiritual, and family dimensions of my life. I haven't succeeded yet, but I'm hard at work.

$$\text{Chapter 2}$$

OUR CALL TO WORK

I don't like work—no man does—but I like what is in work—the chance to find yourself. Your own reality—for yourself, not for others—what no other man can ever know.

JOSEPH CONRAD
HEART OF DARKNESS

According to the story, the story of our beginnings, Genesis, it all began in a garden. God creates a garden, full of fruit, all green and bountiful. God creates the garden, not through work but rather through the Word. God simply speaks, and the world springs forth. Then, "The LORD God took the man and put him in the garden of Eden to till it and keep it" (Gen. 2:15). The creature is given a task to do, assigned as a caretaker of God's good garden. This Hebrew view of humanity as coworker with God contrasts sharply with the thought of the Greeks. Generally speaking, Greeks like Aristotle taught that manual work was demeaning and degrading, not fit for the highest aspirations of humanity.[1]

Then God says, "It is not good that the man should be alone; I will make him a helper as his partner." Thus woman is created. Note that the woman is no secondary, subsidiary creation. She is the advanced, more complicated second attempt by God at human fabrication. She is not the man's servant. She is his partner, his coworker in the garden. "And the man and his wife were both naked, and were not ashamed" (Gen. 2:25). Idyllic, childlike innocence in the good garden is the picture of us in our origins, in the first primordial days of humanity.

The Ambiguity of Work

But things changed. The man and the woman disobeyed God, failed to follow the limits God set over them. In the story, humanity just can't bear limits. They eat the fruit of the forbidden tree,

---

Human Troubles

ℳost human troubles stem from humanity's inability
to stay in one room.

PASCAL

---

attempting to take matters out of God's hands and into their own.
Not content to be creatures, they attempt to be creators unto
themselves, and thereby is life in the idyllic garden thrown into
conflict and confusion. Here is how Genesis narrates the defile-
ment of the garden by the two creatures:

> Now the serpent was more crafty than any other wild animal that
> the LORD God had made. He said to the woman, "Did God say, 'You
> shall not eat from any tree in the garden'?" The woman said to the
> serpent, "We may eat of the fruit of the trees in the garden; but God
> said, 'You shall not eat of the fruit of the tree that is in the middle
> of the garden, nor shall you touch it, or you shall die.'" But the
> serpent said to the woman, "You will not die; for God knows that
> when you eat of it your eyes will be opened, and you will be like God,
> knowing good and evil." So when the woman saw that the tree was
> good for food, and that it was a delight to the eyes, and that the tree
> was to be desired to make one wise, she took of its fruit and ate; and
> she also gave some to her husband, who was with her, and he ate.
> Then the eyes of both were opened, and they knew that they were
> naked; and they sewed fig leaves together and made loincloths for
> themselves.
>   They heard the sound of the LORD God walking in the garden at
> the time of the evening breeze, and the man and his wife hid
> themselves from the presence of the LORD God among the trees of
> the garden. But the LORD God called to the man, and said to him,
> "Where are you?" He said, "I heard the sound of you in the garden,
> and I was afraid, because I was naked; and I hid myself." He said,
> "Who told you that you were naked? Have you eaten from the tree
> of which I commanded you not to eat?" The man said, "The woman
> whom you gave to be with me, she gave me fruit from the tree, and
> I ate." Then the LORD God said to the woman, "What is this that you
> have done?" The woman said, "The serpent tricked me, and I ate."
> The LORD God said to the serpent,

"Because you have done this, / cursed are you among all animals / and among all wild creatures; / upon your belly you shall go, / and dust you shall eat / all the days of your life. / I will put enmity between you and the woman, / and between your offspring and hers; / he will strike your head, / and you will strike his heel." To the woman he said,

"I will greatly increase your pangs in childbearing; / in pain you shall bring forth children, / yet your desire shall be for your husband, / and he shall rule over you." And to the man he said,

"Because you have listened to the voice of your wife, / and have eaten of the tree / about which I commanded you, / 'You shall not eat of it,' / cursed is the ground because of you; / in toil you shall eat of it all the days of your life; / thorns and thistles it shall bring forth for you; / and you shall eat the plants of the field. / By the sweat of your face / you shall eat bread / until you return to the ground, / for out of it you were taken; / you are dust, / and to dust you shall return." (Gen. 3:1-19)

In the beginning, work is good. The creature is graciously invited to share in God's fecundity by being asked to "till and keep" the garden. Furthermore, God being against loneliness, another creature is created to share the man's vocation to "till and keep" the garden. The man and woman are equals, coworkers in community in the garden, those who are urged to be like God and to "be fruitful and multiply," surely one of the most delightful of God's commands.

God-Given Work

God gave man work, not to burden him, but to bless him, and useful work, willingly, cheerfully, effectively done, has always been the finest expression of the human spirit.

WALTER R. COURTENAY

All this changes when the man and the woman eat of the forbidden fruit, succumb to the serpent's urgings, and rebel. They then flee into the bushes, ashamed of their nakedness and vulnerability. They wanted knowledge, wanted to be like gods, wanted to have their eyes opened with new sophistication. Their eyes are opened. But how little they now see! They have gained sophistication and now know only one thing: They are naked and afraid. The ancient storyteller surely means for us to appreciate the irony here. We wanted to grow up, to be like gods, to have unlimited vistas. Our eyes are open and all we see is our genitals!

In the first recorded act of human creativity, we make loincloths for ourselves in a pitiful, human attempt to cover our nakedness, to limit our exposure and vulnerability. In *The Denial of Death* Ernest Becker says that all human creativity, all art, philosophy, architecture, and work have their roots in our futile attempt to cover our nakedness, our human reaction to the awesome truth that we are naked and afraid. We build bridges, skyscrapers, write poetry and books, all in a pitiful attempt to hedge our bets against the awesome curse of death. Work is now related to our main project of countering our vulnerability and nakedness.

Thus the historian Toynbee characterized our work as a means to deal with our innate human anxiety about our lives, an "opiate" which anesthetizes us to the pain of our human vulnerability. Man's work

> saves him from the solitariness that he fears—and his fear is well founded; for when a man is alone he is really alone least of all; he is then naked in the universe; he is face to face with God; and this confrontation is formidable. . . . Modern man . . . takes refuge in anesthetics, and most of all in the opiate of work, which keeps his thoughts away from contemplation by keeping his eyes fixed on the conveyor belt or on the drawing board.[2]

When God returns to the once idyllic garden, encounters the man and woman crouching in the bushes, we see how the once close, familial relationship with God has been destroyed. The God who was once a friend has now become an intruder, a threat, our enemy and accuser.

God questions the man and the woman, and the pitiful blaming begins. Community disintegrates. The man blames his rebellion on the woman, his coworker, and the woman blames it on the snake.

Then God speaks the so-called curse, which is not so much the curse of God as it is the divine enunciation of the results of their rebellion. Now, because of their rebellion, everything is out of balance.

First, the woman is addressed. In an agricultural society, where children were of value for helping do the work of the family and, through carrying on the family name, for being the only means to immortality, children are a blessing. Now, the blessing of childbirth will feel like a curse to the woman. What was once the woman's participation in the joyful creativity of God will now be a source of much pain. The woman, who was created for joyful co-creation with the man, is now dominated by the man.

Women and Work

*P*rimitive and even colonial women played a much more integral role in the business of survival. Their identity as workers and managers was taken for granted. . . . Women were relegated to an inferior caste . . . most dramatically with the coming of industrialization.

MADONNA KOLBENSCHLAG
Kissing Sleeping Beauty Good-Bye

We should note that this state of affairs is *not* what God intended. Male domination is not validated by this story. Rather, male domination of women is clearly represented as sin, as evidence of the ravages of human evil, which has now corrupted community in the once-idyllic garden.

And the man. God tells the man that his work, which was to be his stewardship of the garden, a sharing in God's good garden, will now require great toil and sweat. The dry, stark soil of the Near East stands in marked contrast to the lush garden.[3]

At least a couple of lessons are to be learned from the story of our origins. To be sure, work, our participation in the creativity of God, is a great blessing, a divine summons, a vocation. The various ways in which we are invited to "till and keep" the earth mirror some of the effusive, divine creativity which called the earth into being. Through our labors, the earth keeps being evoked, called into being. Work is a divine gift. Work on the Swedish playhouse by Morfar, Max, and Lucas appears to have been an example of such a gift.

Yet, paradoxically, work has also become a curse. A blessing is what God intended, Genesis seems to say, but a blessing is not what God got. Not content with our limits, we took matters in our own hands and thus despoiled the good garden. Women and men are equal in their struggles to survive in and to live with an often hostile environment. Man struggles to make a living out of the weed-choked, dusty earth; then, when his lifetime ends, he returns to the dust. Woman is enslaved by unjust social structures and labors under the burdens of childbearing.

Any view of work arising out of this primal story is ambiguous at best, somehow mixed with both blessing and curse, which is exactly how most of us experience work. The once-blessed job that demands such creativity of us eventually settles down into boring, grinding routine. In our human efforts at work, we can participate in the very creativity of God, but we can now also terribly despoil our earth home.

The Dark Side of Work

*B*ut work is also capable of creating the dark night—when, for example, our work contributes to the devastation of the planet, to the despair of the young, to hoarding when we ought to be sharing, to control and power games instead of celebrating, to putting people down instead of lifting them up, to injustice instead of justice.

MATTHEW FOX
The Reinvention of Work

No one-sided, reductionistic view of work is permitted by the story. Work can be a blessing. It can be a curse. Human beings work within an ambiguous environment where there are limits. Genesis at least implies that learning to live within the divinely ordained limits is one of the keys to a good life.

God does not desert God's rebellious creatures. One more gift is given to bless their now disordered lives. The Third Commandment offers a day of rest to humanity, a day paralleling the rest which God himself enjoyed at creation (Gen. 2:3).[4]

> Remember the sabbath day, and keep it holy. Six days you shall labor and do all your work. But the seventh day is a sabbath to the LORD your God; you shall not do any work—you, your son or your daughter, your male or female slave, your livestock, or the alien resident in your towns. For in six days the LORD made heaven and earth, the sea, and all that is in them, but rested the seventh day; therefore the LORD blessed the sabbath day and consecrated it. (Exod. 20:8-11)

The sabbath, Israel's unique insight into the nature of life and work, is the mark of an obedient and rightly ordered humanity. The sabbath is set apart as that day of the week when creation is restored to its rightful relationship to God. In the sabbath, time is offered as a gift—as time to worship, to study, and to reflect. In the sabbath, humanity admits that it is not omnipotent, not able to work without end. In the sabbath, humanity experiences the limitation of our work as gift. As Jesus said, "The sabbath was made for humankind" (Mark 2:28). We are not, the sabbath seems to say, created for endless, grinding toil. We are created for intimate, contemplative relationship with God.[5]

The End of Work

*T*he end of work could mean the death of civilization or the beginning of a great social transformation.

JEREMY RIFKIN
Utne Reader[6]

The Protestant Work Ethic

Christians have struggled to be faithful to this biblical view of work as both vocation and punishment, as both blessing and curse. Much has been said of the "Protestant work ethic," a concept which may have been overrated as a significant contributor to our present-day attitudes toward work.

Martin Luther (1483–1546), in his commentary on the passage from Genesis just quoted, says that the story shows "that man was created not for leisure but for work, even in the state of innocence. Therefore the idle sort of life, such as that of monks and nuns, deserves to be condemned."[7] This is obviously not a call to unremitting work, but rather part of Luther's polemic against the monastic orders of his day. Before the Reformation, "vocation" always referred to a call to the monastic life. Luther's attack upon monasticism led to an effort to dignify the work of the common person as somehow divinely ordained. You do not have to become a nun to serve God. Even the lowest servant cleaning the floors in the rich man's house is doing it for the glory of God.

Luther taught that God's creation of the world is dynamic, continuing, new each day. God did not simply create the world and quit. God keeps creating and invites us to participate, in even the humblest of work, in that continuing divine creativity.[8] Thus, Luther's thought on work is not so much an exaltation and glorification of work itself, but rather a way of focusing upon and celebrating the activity of God. Indeed, the modern notion of autonomous humans busily pursuing their own ends would have seemed godless and evil to Luther. When Luther uses "vocation," he uses it more often to refer to our responsibilities like marriage and family than to our jobs. Vocation encompasses the whole of our relationships with the world.[9] Indeed, one can imagine that Luther would be deeply troubled with the modern equation of vocation with occupation. We are called by God, not just in our jobs, but also in marriage, family, leisure, and recreation, to glorify God in all things. Our vocation is not work but worship; we are called to worship God in all that we do.[10]

John Calvin (1509–1564), even more than Luther, praised the work of the common person, expanding the medieval notion of vocation beyond those who were called to be priests or nuns to those engaged in any work that was not dishonest. Calvin wrote that "no task will be so sordid and base, provided you obey your calling in it, that it will not shine and be reckoned very precious in God's sight."[11]

Later Max Weber (1864–1920), a German sociologist, proposed that Protestantism was a leading force behind the growth of capitalism, accusing Calvinism of promoting a kind of Protestant monasticism in which the working classes were told that their work was akin to that of monks and nuns, a new asceticism, a means of salvation.[12] Weber's thesis has been criticized by scholars as simplistic and reductionistic. However, it is undoubtedly true that the Protestant Reformers did alter our view of work, elevating even the meanest job to the status of a divinely ordained call of God, sacralizing secular work as a divine gift and religious obligation. Sometimes, work has been given almost sacramental status, as if God created us for nothing but work rather than also for sabbath rest and worship.[13] After the Reformers, the notion of "call" came to be associated more often with one's job than with, as in the New Testament, obedience to God as a disciple of Christ. While Roman Catholics still speak of a call to a religious order as "having a vocation," today, in secular parlance, "vocation" has come simply to mean your job.[14]

Sometimes the Protestant work ethic contributed to the solidification and defense of indefensible social arrangements. If someone was in a demeaning, degrading job, it was argued, that was because God had put that person there; therefore, that person should not strive for betterment of his or her condition. Luther was fond of citing 1 Corinthians 7:20, "Let each of you remain in the condition in which you were called." Luther used it as a defense of the common, nonmonastic person. One need not leave one's work and join a monastery to serve God. One could serve God where one had been placed. Yet this passage was sometimes used by later interpreters of Luther to mean that God had placed us in certain economic and social situations and that we should content ourselves with our divinely ordained station in life and not venture out of our present situation. Such thought became a powerful hindrance to revolutionary thought and action.

Besides, Luther's assessment was limited by the rather static medieval job situation. Today, the average American young person can expect seven job-changes in his or her lifetime. Many of these job changes will be forced upon the worker by external economic factors. How can these multiple changes, forced upon the worker by market forces from the outside, be called aspects of divine vocation?

Ayn Rand on Work

*P*roductive work is the central purpose of a rational man's life, the central value that integrates and determines the hierarchy of all his other values. Reason is the source, the precondition of his productive work—pride is the result.

AYN RAND

How can it be said that all jobs, regardless of their nature, are vocations from God? Is there some work that, while honest, is so degrading, so demeaning, and so poorly rewarded that it in no way can be called a "vocation"? George MacLeod, founder of the Iona Community of Scotland, often took the job of cleaning the community's latrines so that "I will not be tempted to preach irrelevant sermons on the dignity of all labor."[15] Is leisure and idleness a mark of sinful rebellion against the call of God to work, or is our time of leisure a potential source of rest and renewal akin to the sabbath?

A Christian Critique of Work

Although Protestantism, in its attempt to honor and validate all work as a potential vocation from God, may have contributed to some of the excesses and abuses of capitalism, the Christian and the Jewish faiths also bear within themselves a prophetic critique of work. That critique has its basis in the primal stories of Genesis, in the depiction of work as an ambiguous, potentially evil human phenomenon. Humanity is graciously invited by God to work. The world is not yet finished; there is still work to be done in God's creation, room left for human creativity. Yet our struggles with work, the potentially degrading, dehumanizing aspects of work, are also named in scripture. Jesus has amazingly little to say about work to his disciples. In fact, in the New Testament, the "call" of Jesus appears to be a call to ordinary people like fishermen and tax collectors to leave their secular careers and to follow him on his travels.

Functions of Work

To give a person a chance to utilize and develop his or her faculties; to enable one to overcome one's ego-centeredness by joining with other people in a common task; and to bring forth the goods and services needed for a becoming existence.

E. F. SCHUMACHER
Small Is Beautiful

Thus, while work may be a good gift of God, our present structures of work are not divinely ordained. Work, like any human endeavor—sex, money, art—may be tainted with human sin. For some, that sin will take the form of idolatry—a persistent biblical concern—in which we give honor and energy to our jobs which should be reserved for God. When work becomes the sole purpose of our life, the end toward which all our creativity and energy are directed, work has become an idol, another means of human rebellion against God. Christians have always believed that humanity cannot earn God's love, cannot work out its salvation through its own devices. Our salvation, our relationship to God is a gift of God, not a human achievement. We are saved by God's grace, not by human works.

In his recent encyclical *Laborem Exercens,* Pope John Paul II praises work as "a fundamental dimension of human existence on earth" (9), in which we are graciously invited to be co-creators with God (25).[16] John Paul II makes much of our command to "dominate" the earth, far too much in an era in which we have learned some of the sad ecological results of the glorification of this domination. Genesis says that when God created the world, called it "good," and rested on the seventh day, God thereby proclaimed that creation was complete. Humanity ought to enjoy this creation and to live within its limits; it does not need to co-create. We are to be creatures, not creators or gods unto ourselves.

Furthermore, our work's relationship to materialism and accumulating goods provides another justification for suspicion about our work. The Bible is rather relentless in its attack upon the rich, upon those who gain economic power and use it over others who are less well endowed. Never in the Bible are the poor blamed for their poverty. It is the rich, those who work and accumulate, who are in big trouble. The Hebrew Scriptures show a remarkable concern for economic justice, giving attention to minute details of wages (cf. Jer. 22:13), contracts, and fairness. "You shall not keep for yourself the wages of a laborer until morning" (Lev. 19:13). To be poor and unemployed is clearly a great tragedy in scripture. Presumably, even boring, repetitive assembly-line work is preferable to unemployment. Economic life is more often spoken of as the sphere of sin than as an area of blessing. A gift of God work may be, but it is a frequently perverted gift, according to the Hebrew Scriptures.

Thus when Pope John Paul II speaks of our work as "something worthy, . . . something that corresponds to man's dignity, that expresses this dignity and increases it" (9), the pope is overlooking the way our sin, our rebellion against God, has made our work a deeply problematic affair. Our work is all too rarely an expression of human dignity. Little of our work is inherently, intrinsically

---

"Satisfied Mind"

How many times have you heard someone say
If I had his money, I'd do things my way.
But little they know that it's so hard to find
One rich man in a hundred with a satisfied mind.

PETE SEEGER

fulfilling. Work, if it has great significance for our lives, tends to be symbolic, having value for us because it helps to fulfill some human need other than work.

The Bible thus encourages us to take a critical, humble look at our work. Our present order of work is a human creation and, like any other human creation, can be a source of human perversion, rebellion, and sin. From the beginning, the Genesis writer makes a connection between work and sin. Work is not only something which reflects the creativity of God; work is also a source of deep human conflict. God did not create our present working conditions; we did. Therefore those conditions can and should be changed when they are contrary to the claims of a just and loving God. Can it be said that all work is being done "for the glory of God"? Some claim that we are now living in a "post-vocational age"[17] where faith is trivialized by claims that our faith is the basis of our work. Some work appears to be so boring and repetitive that it is beyond the redemption of our theology. Reflecting on his experience on an assembly line in a French automobile factory, Robert Linhart recalls that

> through the gaps in this gray, gliding line I can glimpse a war of attrition, death versus life and life versus death. Death: being caught up in the line, the imperturbable gliding of the cars, the repetition of identical gesture, the work that's never finished. If one car's done, the next one isn't, and it's already there, unsoldered at the precise spot that's just been done, rough at the precise spot that's just been polished.[18]

Are we giving to our job that which should only be given to God? What are the limits we should expect of ourselves in our work? Because the present work structures are not ordained at creation by God, they can and perhaps should be changed. What changes ought we to make in our patterns of work?

When one takes the Bible as a whole, it must be noted that the Bible is rather remarkably unconcerned about work. Nowhere in the Bible does God call someone to be a fisherman, a farmer, or a servant. When Paul confronts the issue of slaves who have become

---

Four Evils of Industrial Society

*T*here are four main characteristics of modern industrial society which, in the light of the Gospels, must be accounted four great and grievous evils:

1. Its vastly complicated nature.
2. Its continuous stimulation of, and reliance on, the deadly sins of envy and avarice.
3. Its destruction of the content and dignity of most forms of work.
4. Its authoritarian character, owing to organization in excessively large units.

E. F. SCHUMACHER
Good Work

Christians, he tells them, in effect, not to worry much about their present status, not to seek change, because, after all, such matters are not as important as our basic relationship to God. Paul says that we were called, not to various occupations, but rather "to belong to Jesus Christ" (Rom. 1:6). Although Acts 18:3 says that Paul was a tentmaker, it never says that he was called to be one. His vocation was to be an apostle, not a tentmaker (Rom. 1:1). Thus, in the Bible, work is a decidedly secondary vocation. Our relationship to God is based not on our occupation but rather on God's gracious call, and that gracious call is, in the words of the Westminster Confession, not to have a job but rather "to glorify God and enjoy him forever."

The great theologian Karl Barth criticized the modern tendency to equate vocation with occupation, criticizing it as

of a piece with the rather feverish modern over-estimation of work and of the process of production that . . . it should be thought essential to . . . the true nature of man, to have a vocation in this sense. On such a view it is forgotten that there are children and the sick and elderly and others . . . the unemployed . . . [and] innumerable active women who do not have this kind of vocation. . . . We have to remember that for many men the centre of vocation in the material and comprehensive sense is not to be found at the point of their vocation in the narrower sense. . . . A man does not live to work; he works to live.[19]

Pope John Paul II argues that, because Jesus was a carpenter, he thereby dignified physical labor and preached

the most eloquent Gospel of work, showing that the basis for determining the value of human work is not primarily the kind of work being done, but the fact that the one who is doing it is a person. The sources of the dignity of work are to be sought primarily in the subjective dimension, not in the objective one (6).

Christian theologian Stanley Hauerwas notes that (1) the pope's assumption that Jesus was a carpenter has little scriptural basis, and (2) the pope's assertion that no matter how degrading work may be, the "subjective dimension" of the "person" dignifies all work, is a naive romanticism which could serve to legitimate all sorts of inhuman forms of work as long as the person subjectively feels like a "person." Much work is unworthy of too much theological praise.

The pope has thus revived some of the worst aspects of the old Protestant work ethic, romanticizing work and using a too-exalted theology of work which could be perverted to justify work that ought not to be theologically dignified.

Thus this book, and its search for meaning in the workplace, can be said to rest upon some of the foundational assumptions of Jews and Christians about work. We are right to search for meaning in our work, since work is one of the chief tasks given by God to humanity. We are right to be critical of our present structures of work, expecting them to be in need of correction and reform in various ways. Our work, suggests our faith tradition, is the source of great joy, also of much pain. We must, in the words of Barth, learn to work to live, not merely live to work. Making a life is more significant than making a living. Even so, the great Christian writer Dorothy Sayers wrote in her essay "Why Work?" that

work is not, primarily, a thing one does to live, but the thing one lives to do. It is, or should be, the full expression of the worker's faculties, the thing in which he finds spiritual, mental, and bodily satisfaction, and the medium in which he offers himself to God. We should no longer think of work as something that we hastened to get through in order to enjoy our leisure; we should look on our leisure as the period of changed rhythm that refreshed us for the delightful purpose of getting on with our work.[20]

Although these sentiments might be true for the work of an artist like Sayers, can they be applied to all work? As Albert Camus said, "Without work, all life goes rotten, but when work is soulless, life stifles and dies."

We ought therefore to be cautious about claiming too much for our work. Most of the rewards for our work tend to be rather mundane. For one thing, work is a primary means whereby most people are related to other people. We like our work primarily because it is our main social setting. Most of our friends tend to be related, in one way or another, with our work. One of the most dehumanizing aspects of unemployment is the loneliness, the isolation. For most of us, most of our human interaction is through our work. Also, from a Christian perspective, much of our work has merit because, though it is utterly mundane, it contributes to someone else's life. As a mechanic said to one of us recently, "People need me more than they need a brain surgeon. When I put somebody's car back together, they're grateful and I'm happy." Work is the principal way we discover our dependence on one another, our connectedness to a wide web of other persons' work.

For another thing, most of us work for the mundane, but albeit utterly necessary need to earn a living. Our work puts bread on the table. Rather than debate which forms of work contribute to our personhood and which do not, we ought to focus on which work compensates a worker in a fair and just manner and which work doesn't. Therefore, rather than theologizing about work being an important part of our personhood, or the way in which we share in God's creativity, we, as Christians and Jews, ought simply to talk about work as the means whereby we earn a living. There is, in some of our academic, theological talk about work a subtle elitism, which assumes that, in order for work to be worthwhile, it must have some exalted significance. It must contribute to our humanity, our personhood, our creativity, or some other abstraction. This is a mistake. We ought, rather, to admit that on most days, most of us work for pay. While we are working for pay, we can achieve many other noble human goals. But none of those noble purposes should deter us from the most basic idea that all ought to have work and that all ought to be justly compensated for their work. A fair, living wage is more to the point than our high-sounding theological platitudes.

Furthermore, work also gives us something to do with our time. If we did not have to get up and go to work, boredom would be a great problem for us. To say too much more about our work risks making an idol of our work. Again, according to the Genesis story, it might be concluded that most of our human heartache occurs when people think too much of their work, when work becomes inflated as something grand and godlike, when our work is seen, not as a means of keeping busy or putting food on the table, but rather as a pretentious way to "make a name for ourselves" (Gen. 11:4).

Don W. Shriver, Jr., suggests that churches and synagogues need to talk more about our work and what makes work religiously interesting. For too long, our religious communities have tended to hold themselves somewhat remote from where most of us spend our lives from 9 to 5. Shriver suggests that Labor Day Sunday ought to be used for reflection in sermons and services about a Christian view of work.[21]

We must work to improve our work, for the creation story suggests that, in our work, we have the potential to experience some of the same divine joy and exuberant creativity which brought the very world into being—just as we saw in the work of Morfar and his two grandsons on the playhouse. At the same time, we ought to be deeply suspicious about claiming too much for our work, realizing that, from the beginning, human work is a deeply ambiguous, problematic, often idolatrous activity of human beings, who, not content to be God's beloved creatures, seek to become creators ourselves.

Chapter 3

THE MEANING OF WORK

Good living and good working go together. Life and livelihood ought not to be separated but to flow from the same source, which is Spirit. Spirit means life, and both life and livelihood are about living in depth, living with meaning, purpose, joy, and a sense of contributing to the greater community. A spirituality of work is about bringing life and livelihood back together again. And Spirit with them.

MATTHEW FOX
THE REINVENTION OF WORK

The Life Matrix

The search for meaning in the workplace is a twofold problem involving employees and employers. The employee's problem rather obviously is to find meaningful work. But increasingly many employers are assuming more responsibility in helping create a meaningful work environment for their employees.

One of the reasons why many people find meaning in the workplace to be so elusive is that neither employees nor employers understand the choices available to them. To help sort out these options and evaluate their spiritual, intellectual, emotional, and physiological consequences, we employ a simple matrix, which we first introduced in *The Search for Meaning* and call the *life matrix*. It defines four different states of meaning in the workplace: meaninglessness, separation, having, and being. These states are intended to be not rigid, mutually exclusive categories, but rather useful images to help us differentiate among the alternatives from which we may choose. The elements of the matrix represent the likely effects associated with a particular state of meaning. For example, it is not uncommon for someone whose work has no meaning to experience depression, despair, and eventually death.

On a given day one may encounter all four of these states of meaning in one's work—moving from one state to another in response to mood shifts or changes in the workplace environment.

THE LIFE MATRIX

STATES OF MEANING / EFFECTS	MEANINGLESSNESS	SEPARATION	HAVING	BEING
SPIRITUAL	DESPAIR	DETACHMENT	ORTHODOXY	QUEST
INTELLECTUAL	NIHILISM	ALIENATION	HEDONISM	GROWTH
EMOTIONAL	DEPRESSION	ANXIETY	NARCISSISM	BALANCE
PHYSIOLOGICAL	DEATH	SOMATIZATION	HEALTH FETISHISM	HOMEOSTASIS

Some have suggested that separation and meaninglessness are actually statements of the human condition. Having and being are alternative ways of dealing with the pain associated with meaninglessness and separation.

The life matrix is not a quick-fix panacea promising instant gratification in the workplace for those who use it. Rather it is a tool which many managers and employees alike have found helpful, if properly used, in their respective searches. Each of the four states of meaning will now be described in more detail.

Meaninglessness in the Workplace

Many jobs are so boring, repetitive, dangerous, and dehumanizing that they appear to have little or no intrinsic value independent of the product which results. For this reason, the work of dishwashers, street cleaners, sanitation workers, as well as that of filthy, hazardous manufacturing sweatshops, has often been characterized as meaningless. Although society clearly benefits from the smelly, backbreaking work of garbage collectors, the individual worker may find that his or her work provides precious little personal meaning.

In our country, mindless, low-paying jobs are often filled by poor, uneducated workers, many of whom are recent immigrants to the United States. This contrasts sharply with countries like Austria, Sweden, and Switzerland, which, during periods of full employment, pay premium wages to foreign guest workers to do these grubby jobs. With the high rates of unemployment tolerated in our country, marginal workers here are forced to accept such jobs for little pay.

What about prostitutes, pimps, embezzlers, extortionists, gamblers, professional killers, and soldiers of fortune? Is their work meaningful or meaningless? If the government pays you to wage war and kill others in the name of the state, is your work meaningful? What if you produce products such as cigarettes, alcoholic beverages, or carcinogenic chemicals which are hazardous to one's health? Alternatively, what if the production of a particular product involves high personal risk to the company's employees? What is

The Meaninglessness of Work

I undertook great projects: I built houses for myself and planted vineyards. I made gardens and parks and planted all kinds of fruit trees in them. . . . I bought male and female slaves and had other slaves who were born in my house. I also owned more herds and flocks than anyone in Jerusalem before me. I amassed silver and gold for myself, and the treasure of kings and provinces. I acquired men and women singers, and a harem as well—the delights of the heart of man. I became greater by far than anyone in Jerusalem before me. In all this my wisdom stayed with me.

I denied myself nothing my eyes desired; / I refused my heart no pleasure. / My heart took delight in all my work, / and this was the reward for all my labor. / Yet when I surveyed all that my hands had done / and what I had toiled to achieve, / everything was meaningless, a chasing after the wind; / nothing was gained under the sun. . . .

I hated all the things I had toiled for under the sun, because I must leave them to the one who comes after me. And who knows whether he will be a wise man or a fool? Yet he will have control over all the work into which I have poured my effort and skill under the sun. This too is meaningless. So my heart began to despair over all my toilsome labor under the sun. For a man may do his work with wisdom, knowledge and skill, and then he must leave all he owns to someone who has not worked for it. This too is meaningless and a great misfortune. What does a man get for all the toil and anxious striving with which he labors under the sun? All his days his work is pain and grief; even at night his mind does not rest. This too is meaningless.

Ecclesiastes 2:4-11, 18-23 NIV

the meaning of the work of those who sell drugs, continue to make high-tech military weapons even though the Cold War is over, kill endangered species, and destroy rain forests?

If one pursues a career in business, is it possible to have a meaningful career regardless of the nature of the business? Does it matter whether the business is textiles, tobacco, pharmaceuticals, chemicals, plastics, nuclear weapons, or disposable diapers? Are there any differences in the degree of meaningfulness associated with different jobs such as accounting, finance, marketing, production, research and development, and personnel? What about the objectives of the business? Are profit maximization, service, quality, full employment, and good citizenship equally meaningful business objectives?

These are not easy questions. Their answers depend on our personal philosophy—our sense of meaning, our values, our ethical principles, and our sense of social responsibility. For example, if one considers killing a human being to be an act of nihilism, how is it possible to go to work either for a defense contractor or a cigarette manufacturer? If one is opposed to the exploitation of the indigenous people of Central America, how can one support—either explicitly or implicitly—the policies of American companies that contribute to the oppression of these people? Is the design of manipulative television advertisements aimed at Saturday morning cartoon viewers a legitimate vocation for those who derive meaning from children?

Today there are very few products manufactured in America for which there are not at least some adverse social consequences ranging from carcinoma and toxicity to accident-conducive appliances, toys, and automobiles. Finding employment in a business that is consistent with one's sense of meaning is not easy. All too many people are seduced into meaningless jobs by the promise of high salaries and liberal perquisites. The implicit contract offered by many companies is, "In return for your soul, we promise you fame, fortune, and power."

Consider the fifty-year-old engineer who has worked for a large defense contractor for the past twenty years. With the end of the Cold War, he has begun to have increasing doubts about the moral justification for the type of work in which he is engaged. In addition, his job is extremely boring, and he is only rarely consulted by senior management on matters of strategic importance. One day while driving to work, he realizes not only is his secret ambition to become the company president an impossible fantasy, but that he will never move any higher up the corporate ladder. The sheer horror of remaining in the same meaningless job for another twenty years precipitates a severe anxiety attack followed by months of debilitating depression.

Empty Raincoats

We are not destined to be empty raincoats, nameless numbers on a payroll, role occupants, the raw material of economics or sociology, statistics in a government report. If that is to be its price, economic progress is an empty promise. There must be more to life than being a cog in someone else's great machine, hurtling God knows where.

CHARLES HANDY
The Age of Paradox[1]

Many a corporate executive has opted out of corporate life to pursue a quieter, more reflective existence far removed from the executive suite. Often referred to as a "midlife identity crisis," this phenomenon may also be caused by the absence of a sense of purpose or meaning in the lives of these high-level executives. In many firms, senior executives are expected to subscribe to the company's values to advance up the corporate ladder. These values place too much emphasis on greed, the acquisition of power, and the desire to dominate and manipulate others. Motivation comes not from internal personal goals but from recognition and approval by others. This type of behavior eventually results in anxiety, depression, feelings of emptiness, and burnout. Some executives turn to drugs and alcohol to combat their loneliness and emptiness. Thus it is not surprising that there are hundreds of stress-management programs in the United States today. The government estimates that depression costs the United States $43.7 billion a year in lost productivity, absenteeism, and wages.

The Myth of Sisyphus

The Gods had condemned Sisyphus to ceaselessly rolling a rock to the top of a mountain, whence the stone would fall back of its own weight. They had thought with some reason that there is no more dreadful punishment than futile and hopeless labor.

If this myth is tragic, that is because its hero is conscious. Where would his torture be, indeed, if at every step the hope of succeeding upheld him? The workman of today works every day in his life at the same task, and his fate is no less absurd. But it is tragic only at the rare moments when it becomes conscious. Sisyphus, proletarian of the gods, powerless and rebellious, knows the whole extent of his wretched condition: it is what he thinks of during his descent.

ALBERT CAMUS
The Myth of Sisyphus[2]

If we are serious about our quest for meaning in the workplace, then we must confront head-on the very real possibility, illustrated by these examples, that some forms of work are absurd and have no meaning whatsoever. What are some of the consequences of meaningless work? How long can one survive in a meaningless job? The first column of the life matrix depicts some of the spiritual, intellectual, emotional, and physiological effects of meaninglessness in the workplace. If our work has no meaning, can spiritual emptiness and despair be far behind? The price of meaninglessness is nothingness—nihilism, which is more than most souls can tolerate. Spiritual emptiness is a precursor of hopelessness, existential sickness, and eventually physical death.

Joyless Striving

There must be a reason more heart attacks occur between 8:00 and 9:00 a.m. on Monday mornings than at
any other time during the week. There is; it is returning
to work that one hates.

LARRY DOSSEY [3]

But work need not be dangerous, immoral, or demeaning to be
meaningless, as the Pittsburgh TV weathercaster played by Bill
Murray discovered in the movie *Groundhog Day*. Murray finds himself doomed to relive the same day over and over again. Every day
is Groundhog Day, and there literally is no tomorrow. In response
to his plight—or perhaps what is the cause of it—Murray eats too
much, drinks too much, and sleeps around too much. He even tries
unsuccessfully to commit suicide a few times, only to wake up the
next morning on February 2 again.

Unless we come to terms with the fact that our own work may
either be meaningless or could become meaningless, then we are
likely to be drawn to superficial, inadequate sources of meaning
simply because they promise to curb the pain and anxiety associated with the search—a promise not likely to be realized. Consider the biblical book Ecclesiastes, which uses nihilism to
dramatize the question, Does any form of work have meaning?
Or in the words of Albert Camus, "What sordid misery there is
in the condition of a man who works and in a civilization based
on men who work." [4]

The denial of meaninglessness in our work helps explain the
separation and alienation experienced by many of us, as well
as our irresistible attraction to a life based on having. Rather
than deal with the frightening specter of nihilism in the
workplace and all its pain and uncertainty, we try to escape
through narcissism, hedonism, consumerism, and simplistic
religious dogmas and political ideologies, both liberal and
conservative. A firm grasp of nihilism and all its implications is

absolutely essential to the search for meaning in the workplace. There is no escape from the possibility that our work means nothing. On the other hand, meaninglessness does not appear to be a problem for Max, Lucas, and their grandfather in their work on the Swedish playhouse.

Separation and Alienation

Although life may be meaningful, meaning often eludes those in the workplace who are unable to connect with either their inner self, their coworkers, or some source of grounding.

Separation from oneself can be caused by inconsistent parental support, childhood abuse, sexual abuse, religious indoctrination, overindulgence in consumer goods, poverty, and work-related stress. Those who are not in touch with their feelings and do not know who they are often suffer from low self-esteem, anxiety, and even depression, each of which can have a debilitating effect on the quality of one's work. They are easily influenced—often too easily influenced—by their managers and coworkers, spouses, children, and peers. In addition, those who are separated from themselves are frequently lonely, paranoid, and afraid of death, each of which can negatively affect their work.

A second form of separation in the workplace stems from an inability to connect with other people, including one's coworkers. Cathexis (attachment) with other human beings in a hierarchical, authoritarian work environment is very difficult to achieve. Unfulfilled needs for community in the workplace can precipitate feelings of isolation and emptiness as well as spiritual detachment, alienation, anxiety, and somatization (bodily complaints for which there is no evidence of any physiological illness). The conversion of anxiety and stress into bodily symptoms often gives rise to hypochondria as well.

A third type of separation that has implications for the workplace results from a lack of depth or grounding in one's life, leading also to alienation and detachment from one's sense of being.

Mike the Steelworker

Mike is a twenty-year-old steelworker who works for USX (formerly U.S. Steel) in a Pennsylvania steel mill. Mike's grandfather also worked for U.S. Steel and recently retired after working forty years in the same dark, dingy, dangerous, polluting mill. Having grown up in the rural South during the Depression, he and his family experienced real poverty during the 1930s. He quit school when he was sixteen years old to help support the family, but later volunteered for the infantry in World War II.

After the war, Mike's grandfather moved to Pittsburgh where the steel industry was hiring thousands of unskilled workers to meet the postwar demand for steel. His primary aim was to find a stable, secure job to support his family. He recalled the tough times of the 1930s all too well. For forty years he worked on one repetitive—often dangerous—job after another, always doing what he had been told to do and never questioning the authority of his managers.

Throughout the 1950s and 1960s, the hierarchical, authoritarian style of management of U.S. Steel worked very well. The mill where Mike's grandfather worked was one of the most efficient steel mills in the United States. However, the workers and managers alike at U.S. Steel were poorly educated, had grown up in poverty, and had no problem whatsoever working under military-like conditions.

Mike, not unlike his friends Johnny and Sasha in *The Search for Meaning*, has never experienced poverty. When he was born, the standard of living of his family had improved appreciably since the end of the war. His family enjoyed a relatively comfortable middle-class lifestyle. Mike graduated from high school, took some additional courses in the local community college, and watched too much television when he was growing up. He has never been exposed to military service.

Although Mike is well paid, he is grossly overqualified for his monotonous, unchallenging job. He often wonders why a high school degree was required for such mindless work. Mike is not interested in politics and has never registered to vote.

Mike doesn't like to work very hard. Given a choice between more work for more pay and a day off from work, he will always opt for the leisure alternative. Mike resents the heavy-handed, top-down, authoritarian style of management practiced at the mill. He's often late to work and frequently does not show up at all. Mike drinks a lot of beer and sometimes smokes pot on the job. His relationship with women could best be described as promiscuous.

The story of Mike is a story about the dehumanizing aspects of large American industrial companies. Although Mike's grandfather endured boring, repetitive, hazardous jobs for four decades on the basis of ignorance and fear, the same working conditions today produce feelings of alienation, detachment, ambivalence, and complete disaffection—feelings widespread throughout the industrial world. Mike is alienated from his work, his boss, his family, the government, and his basic beliefs. Drug abuse, alcoholism, divorce, sexual abuse, suicide, crime, and violence are all rooted in separation and meaninglessness.

Obviously, the plight of Mike the steelworker is a lot different from the trouble-free life of Max and Lucas, the young Swedish boys, who spend their summers building playhouses. With the loss of so many manufacturing jobs in today's economy, Mike is more likely to work for a fast-food firm such as McDonald's, Burger King, or Kentucky Fried Chicken than for a large manufacturing plant. Indeed, "Mike" is probably "Marge," a woman rather than a man, working for a service sector firm. Unfortunately, the problems of male and female service sector workers differ little from those of Mike the steelworker.

Most American companies, whether they be in the service sector or the industrial sector, employ the same management philosophy and organizational structures today that worked so well for them in the 1950s and 1960s. However, the typical worker in the 1950s was a child of poverty, uneducated, and comfortable with military authority. Today workers like Mike are well-educated, affluent, and resentful of any kind of authority.

Alienation

Alienation stems from separation from oneself, from others, and from one's grounding. Alienation in the workplace is the result of an individual being transformed into a dehumanized thing or object through work itself.

Alienation

*M*odern man has transformed himself into a commodity; he experiences his life energy as an investment with which he should make the highest profit, considering his position and the situation on the personality market. He is alienated from himself, from his fellow men and from nature. His main aim is profitable exchange of his skills, knowledge, and of himself, his "personality package" with others who are equally intent on a fair and profitable exchange. Life has no goal except the one to move, no principle except the one of fair exchange, no satisfaction except the one to consume.

ERICH FROMM
The Art of Loving[5]

According to one pessimistic view, the only way to avoid alienation in the workplace is to be self-employed. Karl Marx said, "A being does not regard himself as independent unless he is his own master, and he is only his own master when he owes his existence to himself. A man who lives by the favor of another considers himself a dependent being."[6] Or in the cogent words of Albert Camus, "There is dignity in work only when it is freely accepted."[7] In our highly organized, mass-production, consumer-driven, capitalistic society, many dream of the possibility of being self-employed. Few succeed at it.

A significant number of college graduates are accepting jobs these days that do not require college degrees. These jobs are often low-wage, dead-end positions with stagnating or declining real wages. For many corporate jobs that require a college degree, the importance of the degree to job performance is often minimal. A surprisingly large number of employees and managers are significantly overeducated for their boring, mindless jobs.

Graduate schools of business have done little to reduce alienation in the workplace. If anything, they may have actually exacerbated the problem. Their attitude toward blue-collar workers is often arrogant and condescending. They are interested in neither Mike nor his problems.

Business schools have not discouraged the "anything goes" attitude which prevails in the corporate executive suite. The new breed of me-first managers trained in graduate schools of business is not uncomfortable with insider-trading, hostile takeovers, bribery of foreign officials, and heavy-handed anti-union tactics. Business schools offer few courses in business ethics or management philosophy.

Unfortunately the problem of alienation is not limited to those who work in business. That colleges and universities are so ineffective in helping their students find meaning in their lives should come as no surprise. Excessive academic professionalism, research grantsmanship, and functional isolationism are evidence of the disarray and absence of community on college campuses. Professors are engaged in an intense competition for promotions, research grants, and their share of a decreasing pool of funds for faculty salary increases.

There is little evidence to suggest that our colleges and universities possess either the will or the leadership to lead our nation beyond the "me" generation of the 1980s. They are an integral part of the problem rather than a catalyst for change. Academic politics appears to be far more important to many faculty members than the care and nurturing of their students.[8]

Fifty years ago a physician was a devoted public servant who called on his patients in their homes, would accept payment in kind (a chicken, a sack of tomatoes, or a fifth of whiskey), and frequently was not paid at all. Today the entire health-care system in America is driven by greed and our intense fear of death. Physicians, private profit-making hospitals, drug companies, and health insurance companies are engaged in a never-ending struggle to extract as much money as possible from patients, employers, and the government. How can a physician work for a for-profit hospital and still be bound by loyalty to the patient? Large health-care conglomer-

ates now provide their customers with a complete range of integrated health services including insurance, pharmaceuticals, other
health-care products, out-patient medical service, hospitalization,
surgery, medical testing, psychiatric care, nursing home and con-
valescence care, hospice care, and funeral services. So-called managed-care medicine combines the very worst features of both
socialized medicine and free-market medicine into one grotesque,
dehumanized system. This is called progress!

Presidents Jimmy Carter, Ronald Reagan, and George Bush
were each elected by running against the federal government in
Washington. The picture they painted of our civil servants was one
of a bunch of incompetent, lazy bureaucrats who suck from the
public till and create nothing of value for society. After sixteen years
of such shabby treatment by their CEO's, it was hardly surprising
to find that the self-esteem of many full-time government officials
had dropped to an all-time low. As a result, dozens of members of
Congress have not sought reelection in the 1990s. When veteran
Arkansas Senator David Pryor decided to leave the Senate, he
indicated that he was "tired" and "discouraged" by the mood of
American politics in general and the Senate in particular. He noted
that the Senate had become a "less civil, less thoughtful place" than
it was when he entered it eighteen years earlier.

Neither Democrats nor the Republicans have a clue to how to
go about solving most of our serious domestic problems. The big
government, tax-and-spend policies of the Democrats have done
little to slow the death spiral of our cities or allay rural poverty. By
usurping the power of state and local governments, the federal
government has suppressed local community initiative and sense
of social responsibility. The Republicans, on the other hand, would
have us believe that the only solution to our problems lies in gutting
the federal government and abolishing most Democrat-supported
programs. Neither party talks very specifically about local responsibility for the solution of neighborhood, village, or farm community problems. The Democrats want the government to assume too
much responsibility; the Republicans hardly any at all. Regardless
of which party is in power, the results are usually the same.

The United States is so large and so diverse that the problems of Los Angeles and Chicago bear little resemblance to those of Texas, Vermont, Oregon, or the Mississippi Delta. People living in Richmond, Virginia, couldn't care less about the problems of Harlem, and vice versa.

Is it any wonder that Congress has so much difficulty reaching a consensus on anything? It is unrealistic for one legislative body to try to represent so many heterogeneous states, ethnic minorities, political ideologies, and religious sects. That gridlock is the rule on Capitol Hill is hardly surprising.

What is conspicuously absent in the United States these days is a well-defined sense of community or feeling of connectedness linking our fifty disjointed states. This is in sharp contrast to smaller countries like Austria, Finland, Norway, Sweden, and Switzerland, which enjoy not only a very high standard of living but a real sense of community.

Labor-Management Conflict

Another factor contributing to the sense of alienation and powerlessness in the workplace is the confrontational nature of labor-management relations in America. The history of the American labor movement is a story of mutually destructive labor-management conflict. The American approach to industrial relations has always been based on a macho zero-sum (my gain is your loss) mind-set, in which management perceived that labor's gains would result in equivalent losses for management. Organized labor's view has been much the same: Labor's gains can be achieved only by imposing comparable costs on management.

Who is to blame for the confrontational labor-management relations which have persisted in this country throughout the twentieth century? There is plenty of blame to share on both sides.

Labor-management relations in Europe are much more participatory and less confrontational than in the United States, reflecting a combination of enlightened corporate and union leadership, as well as extensive legislation protecting the rights of employees.

Although unions in Europe are much stronger than their counterparts in the United States, there are far fewer strikes or significant labor conflicts than in the United States. Unions in Germany, Sweden, Finland, and Austria are very powerful but have leaders who know a great deal about what's going on in the industries they represent. Unlike United States laws, European labor laws are heavily biased in favor of employees. It is for example, very difficult to fire an employee for any reason other than a demonstrable decline in business. Employees have strong legal protection from indiscriminate layoffs.

Competition

*T*here is a large and overwhelming body of evidence demonstrating that competition in human culture, whether it be in business or other endeavors, does not improve the species, but is maladaptive and far from being the most intelligent cultural strategy.

PAUL HAWKEN
Ecology of Commerce [9]

Labor-management relations in Europe are based more on a spirit of cooperation than on conflict. Both corporate managers and labor leaders know the limits of their power and understand that, if the enterprise cannot successfully compete in the international marketplace, then both sides will lose. There is more of a win-win attitude than the divisive zero-sum approach which characterizes American labor-management relations.

We do not mean to imply that employee relations in all American companies are based on distrust and confrontation. Hewlett-Packard, 3M, Intel, Motorola, Southwest Airlines, Delta Air Lines, and United Parcel are among the many companies in the United States which do approach their employees in an enlightened non-confrontational fashion.

Businesses may pay a very high price if their employees cannot find meaning either within the company or in their private lives. Undemocratic, hierarchically organized companies with a confrontational management style are not conducive to the search for meaning or community in the workplace.

Fortunately, separation and alienation are not among the problems little Max and Lucas have to deal with in their work on the Swedish playhouse.

Having

In an attempt to avoid the pain and suffering associated with separation and meaninglessness in the workplace and elsewhere, many of us seek meaning through a life based on having. By owning, possessing, manipulating, and controlling material possessions, wealth, and other people, we hope to find security and certainty in an otherwise uncertain world. Those in the having mode want to hold on to what they've got at any cost. They live by the slogan, "I've got mine, Jack." What life is all about is "looking out for number one."

Legalism, religious orthodoxy, political dogmatism, and labor-management tension are all associated with a personal philosophy based on having. In response to their insatiable psychological and sensory needs, those who are into having often exhibit behavioral patterns which are aggressive, competitive, and confrontational. To have someone or something is to take charge of it or to conquer it. Robbing, killing, overpowering, and consuming are obvious examples of having. Commanding someone to do something in the workplace is also a form of having. Those in the having mode are always afraid they are going to lose what they have.

We are a nation obsessed with having and consuming people and things. We are so preoccupied with having that we have lost our ability to be human beings. Our happiness depends mostly on our superiority to others, on our power, and on our ability to manipulate others. This is particularly true of the workplace. Capitalist America may be the most efficient and productive nation in the world, but it extracts a high human cost.

As we noted in *The Search for Meaning*, for our economy to function, those who are expected to do the work must believe in the American dream, which links happiness to what one owns. The path to happiness involves accumulating enough money or credit so that you can buy a nicely furnished house in a good neighborhood, a couple of cars, a color TV, a boat, and a college education for your kids. To be able to afford all of these things, you must work hard until you retire or die. The harder you work, the more money you will have. And according to this widely accepted script, the more money you have, the more you can buy, and the happier you will be.

Teach Me How to Be a Moneymaking Machine

Schools have failed our individual human needs, supporting fallacious notions of "progress" and development that follow from the belief that ever-increasing production, consumption, and profit are proper yardsticks for measuring the quality of human life. Our universities have become recruiters of personnel for the consumer society, certifying citizens for service, while at the same time disposing of those adjudged unfit for the competitive race.

IVAN ILLICH
Deschooling Society[10]

But if this is true, why are there so many unhappy people in America? Why are the rates of divorce, suicide, abortion, and substance abuse so high, if the American dream is working the way it is supposed to work? Once we have something, does it make us any happier? Does it give meaning to our life?

Repeated public opinion polls conducted over the past four decades suggest that consumerism may not be all that it is cracked up to be. The percentage of Americans claiming to be "very happy" has remained constant over this period at about 33 percent even though personal consumption has doubled.

Our entire economy is based on the illusion that the accumulation of wealth and material possessions can provide meaning to life. The less meaning there is in one's life, the easier it is to be seduced into the materialistic work hard, play hard, be happy syndrome.

Jimmy Carter on Having

*I*n a nation that was proud of hard work, strong families, close-knit communities, and our faith in God, too many of us now tend to worship self-indulgence and consumption. Human identity is no longer defined by what one does, but by what one owns. But we have discovered that owning things and consuming things does not satisfy our longing for meaning. We've learned that piling up material goods cannot fill the emptiness of lives which have no confidence or purpose.

TELEVISED SPEECH
July 15, 1979

To rationalize an economy driven by meaninglessness and greed, economists have devised powerful myths to convince us that for the good of all to be achieved it is only necessary for each of us to act egoistically. That is, if consumers, managers, employees, and stockholders all do their own hedonistic thing, their interests will converge in the long run and society will evolve toward some form of social optimum.

Nothing better illustrates the effects of having than the undemocratic nature of the American workplace. Even though we take pride in the freedom, individual liberty, and democratic nature of our nation, Kirkpatrick Sale has cogently observed that "during the hours that most of us are employed, we forgo most of our basic democratic rights."[11] In most American companies there are no rights to freedom of speech, freedom of assembly, freedom of the press, or due process. One can be fired on the spot at the whim of one's supervisor without any legal recourse whatsoever.

American companies are among the least democratic institutions in the world. In most companies—large or small—only a handful of people have any significant influence over the answers to such fundamental strategic questions as:

1. In which business should we be?
2. What should be our level of commitment to each business?

3. How should we finance our businesses?
4. In which countries should we operate?
5. How should we organize?
6. What should we research and develop?
7. What should we produce?
8. How should we produce?
9. To whom should we sell?
10. How should we sell?

The typical employee has little input into decisions related to such matters as hiring and firing, salaries and wages, fringe benefits, working conditions, mergers, acquisitions, divestitures, and plant closings.

This incongruity between modern employees and the business environment goes a long way toward explaining the increase in absenteeism among industrial employees, declining productivity, and America's weakened competitive position abroad. Undemocratic, hierarchical organizations make community-building in the workplace impossible and discourage the search for meaning. The huge salary gap between the CEO and employees in most companies does little to engender confidence, trust, and community.

In the 1970s American managers often blamed organized labor for our productivity problems. But high unemployment rates and the Reagan administration's antilabor policies rendered organized labor impotent in the 1980s. As evidence of the undemocratic nature of American companies, union membership has declined from 30 percent in the 1970s to only 16 percent in the workplace, in contrast to 60 percent in Austria and 85 percent in Sweden.

Since the end of World War II, the Congress and state legislatures have passed a plethora of statutes aimed at curbing the power of labor unions and making it either illegal or extremely difficult to carry out a successful labor action against an employer. Most states have laws which ban strikes against state and local governments, and it is illegal for federal employees to go out on strike against the U.S. government. While our government vigorously supported the establishment of so-called free labor unions in

Eastern Europe, it was simultaneously doing everything possible to destroy free labor unions in the United States.

Contrary to what we were promised by business leaders, the decline in the American labor movement has not resulted in a corresponding increase in productivity. Blue-collar workers are more alienated than ever. American companies now face even more intense competition from Japan, Pacific Rim nations, and the European Union.

The Ruling Class

*T*he ruling class in our culture is our managers and executives. They are the class of people who drive much of what we do. They control the majority of our resources, they are the heroes of the American dream. We have no royalty, no powerful church. It is the executives of our organizations who have paved our streets with gold.

We have all created this ruling class. We have separated those who manage the work from those who do the work.

PETER BLOCK
Stewardship[12]

Not unrelated to the absence of democracy in Corporate America is the salary gap between CEO's and other employees. While real wages were declining and corporate profits were flat in the 1980s, the salaries of corporate executives were soaring. During the past two decades, the pay of an average worker expressed in constant dollars and adjusted for taxes decreased by 13 percent, while the adjusted pay of the average CEO of a large American company rose more than four times. American CEO's earn 160 times more than an average worker, while their Japanese and German counterparts earn 16 and 21 times more respectively.[13] General Motors' CEO Jack Smith was paid $6.1 million in salary, bonus, and other compensation in 1994. But this amount pales in comparison to the $550 million received by junk-bond king Michael Milken from Drexel Burnham Lambert in a single year. When Sam Walton, founder of Wal-Mart stores, died in 1992, he was the wealthiest person in America—the shares of Wal-Mart stock held collectively by his family were valued at $23 billion.

In their work on the playhouse, Max and Lucas have not yet been exposed to manipulative and controlling work practices.

Being

Some philosophers question whether one's work has either cosmic or intrinsic meaning. In their view, if our work has any meaning whatsoever, then we must create this meaning ourselves through being rather than having. As we pointed out in *The Search for Meaning*, being involves loving, caring, sharing, cooperating, and participating in work communities rather than owning, manipulating, and controlling people and things. Among the possible sources of meaning in the workplace and elsewhere that can be realized only through being are:

1. *Our Creations*—what we accomplish or give back to the world through our creativity.
2. *Personal Relationships*—what we give to and take from the world through our encounters, experiences, and personal relationships
3. *Community*—our integration into and participation in worthwhile groups.
4. *Pain, Suffering, and Death*—our stand toward a fate we cannot change.[14]

As the fourth column of the life matrix suggests, being can lead to spiritual quest, intellectual growth, emotional balance, and physiological homeostasis. Homeostasis refers to the condition which exists when the interdependent elements and functions of the human body are in a state of relatively stable equilibrium. In no sense are we suggesting that being is a physiological cure-all for all ailments. Rather what we are saying is that there is a better

Meaning-Making

We make meaning out of our lives by our intention. It is our intention and willingness to act that makes meaning. Meaning-making encompasses both the present moment and future possibilities—both halves of reality. Our intention creates the meaning of present circumstances and events as well as the invisible future possibilities.

GEORGE LAND AND BETH JARMAN
Break-Point and Beyond [15]

chance for body, mind, and soul to work together in the being mode than is often the case in the having mode.

The story of Max, Lucas, Morfar, and the Swedish playhouse is a story about being. There can be little doubt that Max, Lucas, and their grandfather were into loving, caring, sharing, cooperating, and participating in their spiritually enriching work.

In *Groundhog Day,* TV weathercaster Bill Murray is able to move beyond February 2 only when he rids himself of his selfish, egocentric ways, gives a beggar a hundred-dollar bill, helps some old ladies along the highway, takes up piano, and relates to his girlfriend in a loving, caring way. As Murray lapses into being, his life becomes more meaningful.

Regardless of one's view of Christianity as a religion, the story of Jesus Christ is also a story about someone who was into "being" in his work—loving, caring, sharing, ministering, healing, suffering, and dying on the cross.

The remainder of this book is devoted almost entirely to the question, How can employees and managers alike learn how to be in their work? In the following chapter we examine the challenging problem of trying to create a sense of real community in the workplace. One way to ascertain whether a particular organization encourages its employees and managers in their own search is by examining the enterprise's management philosophy—the sense of meaning, values, ethics, and social responsibility of its managers.

Return from Work

The return from your work must be the satisfaction that work brings you and the world's need of that work. With this, life is heaven, or as near heaven as you can get. Without this—with work which you despise, which bores you, and which the world does not need—this life is hell.

W. E. B. Du Bois

In chapter 5 we define what we mean by management philosophy and provide examples of companies whose philosophy is based on being. Chapters 6 through 10 describe five alternative strategies for finding meaningful work—self-employment, participatory management, value-based management, employee ownership, and reinventing work—each of which is grounded in being. Without exception, each strategy represents an attempt to simulate in the real world workplace an environment similar to that found in the Swedish playhouse project. Finally, we consider the critical role which work plays in the care and nurturing of our soul and in determining whether or not we die happy.

Chapter 4

THE SEARCH FOR COMMUNITY
IN THE WORKPLACE

The essence of any company—its identity—is found in its beliefs, its values, and its stories. I think of a company as a community, a kind of extended family.

TOM CHAPPELL
THE SOUL OF A BUSINESS[1]

No word appears more often today in the literature on corporate human resources and organizational development than *community*. Everyone seems to be talking about the possibility and desirability of creating community in the workplace, but few have ever experienced real community or have any clue about how to go about building a community. What is a community? Is it possible to create a community in a private profit-making business, a government bureaucracy, or a nonprofit school, college, hospital, or charitable organization? How do we know whether a particular business or enterprise is a community or not? How does one go about building community in the workplace? *A community is a partnership of free people committed to the care and nurturing of each other's mind, body, heart, and soul through participatory means.* Despite all the hype about community in the workplace, the gap between managers—who may also be the owners of a business—and the employees is often so great as to preclude the possibility of community. And as we have noted, confrontational labor-management relations do little to establish the kind of trust required to build community in the workplace.

However, in spite of our skepticism about the practical possibilities of achieving community in the workplace, we believe that community is an important goal for those seeking meaning there. About community-building in the workplace, M. Scott Peck once said, "If Utopia is to emerge, it will do so primarily from the world of business."[2] Not unlike the search for meaning, community-building is a slow and arduous process. Many are the obstacles to community—unabashed individualism, narcissism, authoritarianism, excessive inequality, distrust, alienation, competing interests, dependence, and size. Few have succeeded at it, but the potential rewards in the workplace are substantial. Community is about cooperation, sharing, commitment, communication, trust, justice, empowerment, adaptability, and tension reduction—values acclaimed by many but achieved by few.

Benefits of Community

*T*hose few American corporations that manage to convey a genuine sense of community and belonging to their employees are thriving as a consequence.

THOMAS J. PETERS[3]

We now turn our attention to ten defining characteristics of community-building in the workplace:

1. *Shared Vision*—commitment to a shared vision of the future.

2. *Common Values*—identification of common values and objectives.

3. *Boundaries*—definition of the community's boundaries.

4. *Empowerment*—creation of a system of governance and a community decision-making process which empowers all community members.

5. *Responsibility Sharing*—implementation of a community-wide responsibility sharing system.

6. *Growth and Development*—formulation of strategies for spiritual, intellectual, and emotional growth and development as well as physiological well-being.

7. *Tension Reduction*—development of a conflict resolution mechanism to reduce tension among community members

and between the community and those outside community boundaries.

8. *Education*—provision of members with education and training on community values, decision-making, governance, responsibility, growth and development, and tension reduction.

9. *Feedback*—implementation of an adaptive feedback control system which monitors community performance against objectives and adjusts community strategies accordingly.

10. *Friendship*—creation of an environment which encourages friendships to develop among managers, among employees, and between employees and managers.

Among the examples we shall consider to illustrate the characteristics of community are the Swedish playhouse, small Vermont towns and villages, and Rhino Foods. Rhino Foods is a small specialty frozen dessert, ice-cream novelty, and ice-cream ingredient manufacturer located in Burlington, Vermont, whose sixty employees enjoy a strong sense of community. Rhino promotes a so-called dual bottom line of profitability and social responsibility and has received national attention for its innovative employee exchange program—Rhino's alternative to market-driven employee layoffs.

Shared Vision

Perhaps the single most important element of a real community is the commitment by its members to a *shared vision* of the future. There must be a consensus among members on the answer to the question, What does the community want to be when it grows up? It may be one thing for Tom Chappell, founder and CEO of the natural toothpaste company Tom's of Maine, to say, "We believe our company can be financially successful while behaving in a socially responsible and environmentally sensitive manner." But it is quite another thing for the hundred or so employees of the company to be committed to the same vision of the future.

> *Axiom 1:* If you don't know where you are going, no road will get you there.

The failure to reach agreement on the group's mission has led to the demise of many a would-be community. If management's vision of the future is grounded entirely on profits, stock options, executive bonuses, and special privileges, then community is impossible to achieve with a group of employees in search of job security, higher wages, and increased fringe benefits. Management and labor don't even speak the same language. The most clever organizational development consultant could not create community in such a divisive, zero-sum environment. Community is about cooperation, not the achievement of mutually incompatible, unachievable wish lists.

> *Rhino Foods*
>
> *R*hino Foods is a company whose actions are inspired by the spirit of discovery, innovation, and creativity. Our purpose is to impact the manner in which business is done.

In the words of Ted Castle, president and founder of Rhino Foods,

> Community is never easy. It has to come from the heart. We struggle with it constantly—we live and breathe community.

At Rhino's the employees are organized in teams, which play work-based games for which there are prizes and awards for "winning." Successes and team victories are always "celebrated."

Recall that Morfar, Max, and Lucas celebrated the completion of the playhouse by raising the Swedish flag. At many Japanese companies employees begin their workday by singing the company song.

A Sense of Connection

$\mathcal{W}$e are not meant to stand alone. We need to belong to something or someone. Only where there is mutual commitment will you find people prepared to deny themselves for the good of others.

Loneliness may be the real disease of the next century, as we live alone, work alone, and play alone, insulated by our modem, our Walkman, or our television.

It is no longer clear where we connect or to where we belong. If, however, we belong to nothing, the point of striving is hard to see.

CHARLES HANDY
The Age of Paradox[4]

Common Values

Shared *common values* are another important characteristic of community. In workplace communities, employees and managers alike view themselves as parts of an integrated whole pursuing a common mission which is consistent with their own personal values. If there is nothing more to the business or the organization than each individual's looking out only for his or her self-interest, then community will never be.

Axiom 2: If you fear separation, meaninglessness, and death, then unite.

Cooperation, trust, and human empathy are among the shared values which are vital to the formation and survival of communities. But the integration of such values into the workplace may be a slow and arduous process. Swiss and Austrian Alpine villages which embrace these values did not become communities overnight.

Rather they have evolved over hundreds of years. Many small New England towns and villages committed to individualism, hard work, resourcefulness, versatility, and inventiveness are more than two hundred years old. Places like Middlebury, Brattleboro, and Woodstock in Vermont and New London, New Hampshire, possess many of the characteristics we associate with real communities.

We are skeptical of organizational development consultants and "I'm OK, you're OK" spiritual swamis who claim they can lead groups of thirty to sixty persons into community through weekend community-building workshops. We believe that the results of such attempts at instant community-building are more likely to be pseudocommunity—pretend community—rather than enduring community. There are no shortcuts to community. We all say we want community, but do we want to risk the time and energy that community requires? Are we prepared to pay the price—our cherished individualism—necessary to sustain community?

> *Axiom 3:* The price of community is our unabashed individualism.

The typical New England town has a town hall, a school, a church, a post office, a general store or two, a country inn, and possibly a country fair or a summer festival. More often than not, the school, the church, and the traditional town meeting provide the spiritual glue which holds the community together. Where is the spiritual glue which binds a workplace community? Is it money, job security, the workplace environment, personal relationships, or the work itself?

Jerry Greenfield, cofounder of Ben & Jerry's ice cream, created a new employee committee known as the Joy Gang, reflecting Greenfield's philosophy, "If it's not fun, why do it?" The Joy Gang meets periodically to come up with innovative ways to instill more joy into the workplace at Ben & Jerry's. The Joy Gang has been responsible for introducing a stereo system to provide rock music for production workers, a company song, costume contests, frequent employee celebrations, lunch-hour cookouts, and periodic visits of a masseuse to provide free massages.

Boundaries

In every community there is a continuing tension between the group's need for *exclusivity* on the one hand and the desire for *inclusiveness* on the other hand. Just as a village with no entry restrictions soon becomes a town, and a town without real estate zoning laws evolves into a sprawling metropolis, so too may a small business evolve into a large company and eventually become an unmanageable behemoth such as General Motors or IBM—neither of which is likely to be viewed as a community. A workplace without boundaries will not remain a community very long.

One of the reasons the Swedish playhouse project worked so well is that it had very clearly defined boundaries with regard to space, participation, and time. At Rhino Foods, Ted Castle feels that team membership should not be cost-free—easy come, easy go. Associated with participation on a team should be responsibility sharing and well-defined performance expectations. Teams, too, require limits and boundaries.

The Age of Bigness

On a small scale, everything becomes flexible, healthy, manageable, and delightful, even a baby's ferocious bite. On a large scale everything becomes unstable and assumes the proportions of terror, even the good. Love turns into possessiveness; freedom into tyranny. Harmony, based on the interplay of countless different, little, and vivacious individual actions, is replaced by unity, based on magnetized rigidity and maintained by laborious co-ordination and organization. This is why the great hero of the age of bigness is neither the artist, nor the philosopher, nor the lover. It is the great organizer.

LEOPOLD KOHR
The Breakdown of Nations [5]

Kirkpatrick Sale in his book *Human Scale* has compiled considerable evidence to suggest that sheer size alone is a very important determinant of the long-term viability of a human community. Sale believes there is a size limit beyond which a community should not be allowed to grow if it is to survive. Indeed, it's hard to imagine a workplace community consisting of more than a few hundred employees. Obviously it is much easier to control the growth of a privately owned business than that of a large publicly held enterprise.

Exclusivity is particularly important during the early stages of a growing community to ensure commitment to shared vision, values, and objectives. Rapid organizational growth is incompatible with a stable, enduring workplace community. Mature communities often impose *boundaries* to limit community growth while simultaneously helping nonmembers organize similar communities.

One of the reasons the state of Vermont with its two hundred and fifty or so small towns works so well is that it is small—not unlike Austria, Denmark, Finland, Norway, Sweden, and Switzerland. With only 585,000 inhabitants, most of whom live either in the countryside or in small towns, Vermont is ranked 49th among the 50 states in population—one fiftieth the size of California.

> *Axiom 4:* Keep it simple—always make molehills out of mountains.

Some organizations create artificial barriers to community based on race, religion, or national origin. Others use titles and labels to separate the management class from the working class: manager/employee, nonunion/union, exempt/nonexempt, and salaried/hourly. Boundaries of this type are hardly conducive to community-building.

Whether or not a workplace community survives may depend on how it balances its mutually contradictory dual needs for exclusivity and inclusiveness. One without the other will surely result in failure.

Watching Others Work

We have intentionally structured our organizations so as to exclude lower levels of an organization, those doing the core work, from planning, organizing, and controlling their own work. We admonish managers to put down their calculators, take off their lab coats, put on a tie, and get to the business of watching others work.

PETER BLOCK
Stewardship[6]

Axiom 5: Small is beautiful.

Empowerment

Perhaps the most troublesome attribute of a workplace community is *empowerment*—the right of each employee to share equally the ability to influence and shape the direction of the organization. Every community member is a leader.

Unfortunately, many corporate managers are into having—owning, manipulating, and controlling money, power, people, and things. In response to their insatiable psychological need to be in control, those who are into having often exhibit behavioral patterns which are aggressive, competitive, and antagonistic. To have someone is to take charge of that person—to control him or her. Those in the having mode are afraid of losing what they have to someone else.

Axiom 6: Share power—one person, one vote.

Power sharing may be very threatening to corporate managers, union leaders, and leaders of organizations aspiring to become workplace communities. For an organization to have the possibility of becoming a true community, its leaders must be prepared to risk complete loss of control. This is a higher price than most corporate executives are prepared to pay. This also gets to the crux of why there are precious few workplace communities. As former Soviet Union leader Mikhail S. Gorbachev learned the hard way, *power sharing is very risky business.*

When its principal business, chocolate chip cookie dough, took an unexpected dip in 1993, Ted Castle turned to the employees at Rhino Foods with the question, "Which do you prefer—layoffs, reduced hours and reduced pay, or temporary job sharing with another firm?" They opted for job sharing, in which a dozen or so of Rhino's employees were temporarily assigned to positions with nearby firms. The approach of Rhino's management was that this was the employees' issue and that they should play a strong role in deciding what should be done in response to the temporary crisis.

Axiom 7: There is no daddy (mommy), but if there is a daddy (mommy), he (she) is you.

MARTIN SHUBIK

Some company CEO's naively believe that community can be mandated by executive fiat. Community cannot be ordered from above. Top-down community-building initiatives are perceived by employees as deceptive attempts by management to manipulate them. The primary reason that Soviet-style communism failed was that it tried unsuccessfully to impose community on the Soviet people against their will. That affirmative action racial and male-female quotas have met such strong resistance in the United States is hardly surprising, since they represent an overt attempt by the U.S. government to impose community in the workplace.

Workplace communities must also be grounded on a foundation of *equality* and *justice.* We are not suggesting that all community members must think and act alike. Honest differences of opinion can energize the community and provide a source of creative tension. Members need not have the same level of income or wealth either. But there cannot be huge disparities among members with regard to the fundamental criteria on which the community is

Empowering Me by Empowering You

Empowering Adam by empowering Eve
Empowering the parent by empowering the child
Empowering the teacher by empowering the student
Empowering the physician by empowering the patient
Empowering the therapist by empowering the client
Empowering the priest by empowering the parishioner
Empowering the manager by empowering the employee
Empowering the business by empowering the customer
Empowering the leader by empowering the community
Empowering the city by empowering the neighborhood
Empowering the state by empowering the people
Empowering the strong by empowering the weak
Empowering the rich by empowering the poor
Empowering the righteous by empowering the wicked
Empowering God by empowering us all

THOMAS H. NAYLOR

based, whether the criteria be economic level, profession, crafts-manship, artistic talent, or technical proficiency. A workplace community will not flourish if it is dominated by a handful of people possessing a disproportionate amount of power and influence.

On a small scale, Morfar and his grandsons experienced some of the important elements of power sharing, justice, and equality. For those who choose to avail themselves of the opportunity, New England town meetings are a form of community power sharing. Unfortunately, attendance at Vermont town meetings has been on the wane in recent years, thus providing increased power to a disproportionate few.

Responsibility Sharing

The flip side of power sharing in the workplace is responsibility sharing. Community members should be prepared to share the

Tom's of Maine

In honoring the whole person we have chosen to form a community that is both hierarchical and egalitarian. We want to compete in the marketplace, but we think we can compete better from a foundation of humanness, from shared values. A community, we think, provides the fertile soil that will help us grow, reaching, like Jack's beanstalk, into the sky for more and more market share.

Tom Chappell
The Soul of a Business[7]

responsibility and accountability for achieving the community's goals and objectives. Responsibility sharing implies a very strong commitment to workplace cooperation, participation, and team-building. The group takes on more importance than the individual manager or employee in workplace communities.

Axiom 8: There is no substitute for commitment and hard work.

The very essence of our free enterprise capitalistic system involves promoting the virtues of individualism—often subordinating the interests of the community to those of the individual. The Japanese, on the other hand, take a quite different view of the relationship between the individual and the community. In Japanese companies, for example, the interests of the CEO are subordinated to those of the employees and the customers. The well-being of the group or the community always takes precedence over individual self-interest.

Several years ago after the crash of a Nippon Airlines Boeing 747, which killed several hundred passengers, the CEO of Nippon took personal responsibility for the crash, apologized to the families of those who had been killed, and resigned. One cannot even conceive of the possibility of such an act of contrition on the part of the president of an American airline under similar circumstances. In a typical airline crash in America, the airline, the aircraft manufacturer, the pilots, and the FAA all point the finger of blame at someone other than themselves.

Cost Effectiveness

*B*usiness will adopt community as a standard mode of operation for the sole reason that community is cost-effective.

M. SCOTT PECK
A World Waiting to Be Born[8]

The responsibility for locating, designing, sawing, hammering, and painting the Swedish playhouse was shared equally among Morfar, Max, and Lucas. Responsibility sharing is encouraged in Vermont by the severity of the winters. Rhino Foods has an employees' "wants program." Employees help each other get what each wants through responsibility sharing. Both the employees and the company benefit from the results.

Growth and Development

According to Rolf Österberg, "the primary purpose of a company—its meaning—is to serve as an arena or vehicle for the personal and human development of those who are working in the company."[9] The production of goods and services and the profit which results from the work are by-products of the process, not ends unto themselves.

Axiom 9: Grow spiritually, intellectually, and emotionally or die.

Since none of us lives by bread alone, a viable workplace community must embrace strategies for spiritual, intellectual, and emotional growth and development as well as physiological well-being. There can be little doubt that Morfar and his two grandsons grew emotionally and spiritually while working on the playhouse.

Reality Test

*I*t's a whole lot easier to be concerned about employees' growth and development when you are profitable than when you are not.

TED CASTLE
Rhino Foods

Alienation and distrust are obviously big obstacles to community in the workplace. Competing interests among members can also lead to a breakdown of community. If the real agenda of members is increased personal power and prosperity rather than the well-being of the community, the group will not remain a community for very long. Sustaining the interest and commitment of members, when they are constantly bombarded by external stimuli provided by politicians, the media, peers, and the like, is a formidable challenge to any community.

Excessive psychological dependence on the group leader or guru can also precipitate the premature death of a community. To launch a workplace community often requires a charismatic leader. When members become so attached to the leader that they cannot let go, however, community degenerates into a cult of personality.

Tension Reduction

Two other interrelated features of communities are *adaptability* and *conflict resolution*. An enduring workplace community must be able to adapt to a rapidly changing economic, social, and political environment. Individual community members must be consulted before any significant changes are made in business policies or strategies. And when policy changes do occur, they often benefit from consultation with the entire group, not from the macho, shoot-from-the-hip opinion of an isolated, traditional autocratic leader. Community decision making is deliberate and time-consuming, but it allows members to carefully process critical factors affecting the business.

Just as communities must adapt to environmental changes, so too must they resolve their own internal conflicts as well as those outside the community. Each workplace community needs some sort of conflict resolution mechanism to reduce tension when internal disputes arise among individual community members, as well as when disputes occur with those outside the workplace—customers, investors, suppliers, competitors, and government.

Axiom 10: Reduce tension; don't escalate conflict.

In all too many American companies, management has consistently taken an adversarial stance against competitors, government, and employees—particularly employees belonging to a labor union. And labor leaders have engaged in similar behavior themselves. There is no place for this type of destructive thinking in a workplace community. In a workplace devoted to community-building, a zero-sum mind-set soon gives way to a "win-win" approach to problem solving and conflict resolution. The Swedish playhouse team members resolved their differences through negotiation, not confrontation.

Axiom 11: Might doesn't make right.

Education

Notwithstanding the many virtues of community, life in a workplace community is not without blemishes. Although a small factory or a workplace may be homogeneous and close-knit, it may also be parochial, conservative, resistant to change, and suspicious of outsiders. There is often a low tolerance for nonconformity and opinions that differ from the community norm. Invasion of privacy and nosiness are not uncommon in workplace communities. Rarely are envy, greed, and competitiveness absent from such groups.

Even though one may work in a community, one may still find oneself detached and estranged from other community members. Such experiences may evoke the sentiment "If community life is so great, then why do I feel so bad?"

For all of these reasons, it behooves the community to have an effective *education* and *training* program to teach members community values, decision making, governance, responsibility, growth and development, power sharing, and tension reduction.

Feedback

Finally, a viable workplace community needs some type of *adaptive feedback control system,* which monitors community performance against objectives and adjusts community strategies accordingly. Community-building is very tough business. It requires constant feedback and evaluation. It should come as no surprise that power sharing, responsibility sharing, team building, and participatory management must be continuously sold and resold. In most firms neither labor nor management is accustomed to this type of thinking. Both require considerable training, coaching, and monitoring.

Community Renewal

Community-conscious organizations hold regular renewal sessions, involving as large a portion of the staff as possible, to improve teamwork, clarify values, and review and recommit to the organization's vision and mission. At these enclaves, retelling corporate history and celebrating corporate milestones aid in the bonding process.

CAROLYN R. SHAFFER AND KRISTIN ANUNDSEN
Creating Community Anywhere [10]

Any business or organization contemplating the creation of a workplace community should be fully aware of the endless perils of workplace democracy. Participatory management is a much more difficult form of management than authoritarian management. If management can get by with it, ordering someone to do something is much easier than trying to have a group of employees reach a consensus on a particular action. The only problem is that well-educated, affluent employees like Mike the steelworker resent being told what to do by anyone. Therein lies the rub.

> *Axiom 12:* Cooperate and communicate, if you want to survive.

To add insult to injury, some employees react negatively to their new-found options in the workplace. They simply do not want the additional responsibility. They would rather be told what to do than get involved in the decision-making process.

Under the most ideal circumstances, community-building in the workplace is slow and tedious. The risk of failure is substantial. But the possible benefits include improved morale, reduced absenteeism, increased productivity, and more meaningful lives for all concerned.

Friendship

Spiritual guru Thomas Moore, author of *Care of the Soul* and *Soul Mates,* has some cogent advice for those seeking meaningful work. Moore suggests asking a prospective employer, "How easy is it to make friends in your company?"

Community is about personal relationships. The workplace should foster friendship among employees, among managers, and between managers and employees. Morfar, Lucas, and Max were not only related by blood, but they became very good friends as well. Rhino Foods' relationship with its employees is "founded upon a climate of mutual trust and respect within an environment for listening and personal expression." It claims that it is a vehicle for its people becoming friends and getting what they want. Without friendship there can be little joy and little meaning in the workplace.

As we said in *The Search for Meaning*, the reason community is so important to those of us involved in the quest for meaning stems from the specter of separation, meaninglessness, and death. We know that we are separated from ourselves, others, and the ground of our being. We are also haunted by the deep and lingering fear that our life may have no meaning at all. As if separation and meaninglessness were not enough for a poor soul to bear, we must also deal with the uncertainty and apparent nothingness of our own death.

A workplace community is a continuing laboratory test-site for life, love, friendship, work, meaning, soul crafting, and death. In community, we receive encouragement and guidance from our friends for our search. It can also be a source of fun, fellowship, humor, and great joy for the young and the old, the rich and the poor, the educated and the uneducated.

We believe that community not only can reduce our separateness, but it can also facilitate our search for meaning and help us come to terms with our finiteness. Through the workplace community we can close some of the gaps which separate us and work together to seek meaning, confronting our common plight, namely death. Community is one of the most important openings to our soul—a window of opportunity for a happy death—a way to make friends.

Chapter 5

MANAGEMENT PHILOSOPHY

The ultimate purpose of business is not, or should not be, simply to make money. Nor is it merely a system of making and selling things. The promise of business is to increase the general well-being of humankind through service, a creative invention and ethical philosophy. Making money is totally meaningless, an insufficient pursuit for the complex and decaying world we live in.

PAUL HAWKEN
THE ECOLOGY OF COMMERCE[1]

What seems to be missing from many American companies is a well-defined sense of direction for management that goes beyond narrowly defined financial targets. Are there reasons other than simply maximizing shareholders' wealth as to why an enterprise should exist in the first place? Is it important to communicate management's sense of purpose, values, and ethical principles to employees, customers, suppliers, shareholders, and the public? An increasing number of successful companies such as Avis, Ben & Jerry's, Hewlett-Packard, Johnson and Johnson, and Pax World Fund seem to think the answer to this question is yes. These companies have all devised formal statements of management philosophy.[2]

A philosophy of management is concerned with the fundamental principles on which the affairs of a business are based. It should capture the sense of meaning and direction of the management. A well-thought-out management philosophy will have significant impact on the company's goals, objectives, strategies, and policies as well as the corporate culture and style of management. Not unlike a personal philosophy, a management philosophy is a mirror image of the heart and soul of management. It defines the core of management's existence. It should provide a clear signal to employees as to what the business is all about.

Because of the lack of a rudder, it is not surprising to find a number of corporate ships floundering aimlessly in a sea of economic chaos. Corporations whose leaders have no clearly defined sense of meaning or direction in their personal lives have great difficulty motivating employees on board a leaderless ship.

Justice Brandeis on Business

*R*eal success in business is to be found in achievements comparable rather with those of the artist or the scientist, of the inventor or the statesman. And the joys sought in the profession of business must be like their joys and not the vulgar satisfaction which is experienced in the acquisition of money, in the exercise of power, or in the frivolous pleasure of mere winning.

JUSTICE LOUIS BRANDEIS

The senior management of every company—large or small—has a management philosophy. In most cases it has never been formally written down on a sheet of paper for circulation to the employees. Instead, it exists only in the mind of the company's CEO. Few senior executives have taken the time or effort required to draft a formal management philosophy.

There are several reasons why it may be beneficial for senior management to devise a formal statement of philosophy. Very often when top management attempts to reach a consensus over its philosophy, different managers have radically different understandings of one another's fundamental principles.

When there is no written statement spelling out management's basic principles, honest differences of opinion may go unnoticed for a long time; and may be difficult to resolve when they do come to light. Furthermore, the limitations of unwritten communications become more obvious the larger the company becomes.

Later-generation employees who have never met the founder may have only a distorted view of the founder's original vision of the company. The older the company becomes and the more removed it is from the founder, the more important it is to have a written version of the management's philosophy.

The Publix Philosophy

*A*t Publix we believe our primary responsibility is to operate the best stores possible, where shopping and working are always a pleasure and where the customer is always provided with fair values.

In order to accomplish this objective, Publix people must be willing to commit themselves

—to pursue, aggressively, increased sales in all departments by giving our customers friendly helpful service, by offering top quality merchandise at a fair price, and by keeping our stores and facilities clean and neat and in a condition that reflects the pride of Publix people;

—to emphasize value in all aspects of our business, both in products and in service;

—to recognize the highest level of legal, ethical, and social standards;

—to hire and promote people who are committed to being the best in our line of work;

—to be totally fair and honest with all people—customers, employees, suppliers, and shareholders;

—to prove that friendliness is compatible with efficiency and that quality is consistent with a reasonable price.

We believe that if we sincerely follow these fundamentals with honesty, fairness, and integrity, we will achieve dynamic growth, earn a fair profit, and continue to set the Standard for Excellence in the supermarket industry.

PUBLIX SUPERMARKETS
Lakeland, Florida

The absence of a well-defined philosophy implies a certain lack of discipline on the part of top management. It shows a lack of commitment to a specific set of principles. This void soon becomes obvious to all of the company's other managers and employees. Such a company is an easy target for its external environment including competitors, customers, and politicians.

A meaningful management philosophy should address the questions: What does the company do *for people?* What does it do *to people?* How do *people participate* in the business activities of the company? Not surprisingly, the elements of a management philosophy are very similar to those of a personal philosophy: (1) a sense of meaning, (2) a statement of values, (3) ethical principles, and (4) a statement of corporate responsibility.[3] It is important to note that managers and employees—not companies—have philosophies of management.

Before plunging into the formulation of a management philosophy for your own organization, some readers may find it useful to apply these concepts to the idyllic case of the Swedish playhouse project. Specifically, we suggest that you try to articulate the sense of meaning, values, ethics, and social responsibility of Max, Lucas, and Morfar.

Sense of Meaning

One of the most difficult steps for a manager in formulating a management philosophy lies in expressing his or her sense of meaning as related to the business. Few managers are very comfortable in sharing their views on the meaning of their business life with their colleagues. Often one has to resort to indirect means to encourage managers to articulate their feelings on what their business life actually means to them.

Obviously, if a manager has no *sense of meaning,* then formulating a management philosophy is impossible. But the very act of trying to write such a piece may help management come to terms with some of its existential anxieties and meaninglessness. Arguably there is meaning in the search itself, and writing is a critical part of the search process.

A useful beginning involves having each member of the senior management team write a short work history outlining the most meaningful events in his or her work life—particularly as related to your specific company or organization. For examples, recall that each coauthor of this book presented his respective work history in chapter 1. Such a history should attempt to capture those occurrences in one's work life which have provided the most meaning: personal encounters, business crises, as well as personal successes and failures.

Next each manager involved in formulating the organization's management philosophy must confront the following tough questions:

1. Who are we and what is this organization about?
2. Where are we going?
3. How can we prevent our lives together from being a series of accidents?
4. What do we want to be when we grow up?
5. As managers are we separated from one another, our employees, or the ground of our being?
6. Are we into having—owning, possessing, and controlling people, things, and material wealth?
7. Or do we prefer to be into being—caring, sharing, cooperating, and participating?
8. Is our work together meaningful?
9. Is our workplace a community?
10. Can we die happy working for this organization?

The answers to these questions as well as the meaningful events reported in each manager's work history, can be used to compile an initial exhaustive, shoot-from-the-hip list of possible sources of meaning for the entire senior management team. With the help of an outside facilitator, the list is then pared down so that it includes only those activities and events which are *most* meaningful to senior management. Once there is a consensus among the managers on the list, someone on the team—possibly the CEO—should write a narrative statement summarizing the essence of the list. Team members should have the opportunity to craft the wording of the piece and make changes in it. If there is no agreement among the managers, there is little chance of getting the employees to buy into the sense of meaning statement. Such a statement is clearly an evolving document, one that may require repeated evaluation and refinement. Depending on the response of employees to the statement, even further refinements in the statement may be needed.

To bring all of this down to earth, try to articulate the sense of meaning of Morfar and his two grandsons as they built the playhouse on the Swedish island. Was there any tension between having and being in the story? How important were creativity, personal relationships, and sense of community?

Mission: Impossible?

*I*n our increasingly frantic search for meaning, how can companies make sure they and their employees are traveling the same path?

MARGARET KAETER
Business Ethics[4]

No matter how elusive the search for meaning may be, it behooves management to give considerable thought to how it can create an environment that encourages managers and employees alike to find meaning in their individual lives. There are no quick-and-easy answers to questions related to life's meaning, but organizations should be aware of and recognize the importance of this subject to the mental health of their employees. Although corporations are not in the meaning business, it is an act of irresponsibility for an organization to stifle its employees' quest for meaning.

Statement of Values

Once management has expressed its sense of meaning, it may then consider the question of basic managerial *values*. Values are social principles or standards by which we judge ourselves. Our values are strongly influenced by our sense of meaning and vice versa. Values reflect the importance of the spiritual, intellectual, emotional, and physiological dimensions of our life. Among the values which often appear in statements of values are justice, equity, liberty, love, efficiency, fidelity, loyalty, gratitude, beneficence, and self-improvement.

As was the case with management's sense of meaning, a facilitator may also prove to be useful in helping management articulate its values. Psychologists, theologians, and philosophers have been used as effective catalysts to the process of value formulation. Many companies find that a two-day off-site retreat is particularly conducive to producing a management philosophy. Obviously, arriving at a consensus on corporate values may take considerable effort if the management group is relatively heterogeneous with respect to values. Indeed, there is a risk of creating a rift among managers if serious value differences come to the surface.

The problem is further confounded if one attempts to involve all the employees in the workplace in the value-defining process. If a company has only a few hundred employees, then it may be possible through employee surveys and employee teams and committees to obtain employee input on values as well as the other elements of an evolving management philosophy. But if a company has tens of thousands of employees, their participation in the process of formulating a management philosophy becomes quite problematic. Size alone is indeed a big obstacle to participatory management practices. Big governments, big companies, big labor unions, big cities, big churches, and big universities are rarely very democratic.

Bigness

There seems only one cause behind all forms of social misery: *bigness*. It appears to be the one and only problem permeating all creation. Whenever something is wrong, something is too big.

LEOPOLD KOHR
The Breakdown of Nations[5]

What values did Max, Lucas, and Morfar share as they built the playhouse together?

Values

*V*alues are like organizational DNA. They tell people how to act. They also set the first stage for helping employees decide if a company is the right place for them.

MARGARET KAETER
Business Ethics[6]

Not unlike management's sense of meaning, the development of a statement of values is also an evolutionary process. We may begin this process by compiling a long list of, say, fifteen or twenty possible values. Some of these values may either be redundant, inconsistent with one another, or incompatible with the management team's sense of meaning and can, therefore, be deleted from the list. The final list of values should probably contain no more than five or six values to which management is seriously committed.

The MBA

*W*e train the managerial class in our MBA programs. If you do not believe this ask the graduates of MBA programs about their expectations. They want to start at the top, and move up from there.

PETER BLOCK
Stewardship[7]

If a company's management philosophy contains too many values, then they may not be taken seriously by the employees. Management may be perceived by some as trying to be all things to all people. It is better to go with a shorter list of values in which you truly believe, than to misrepresent the values of management. For years IBM has espoused only three values—respect for the individual, customer service, and excellence.

The Avis Quest for Excellence

*A*t Avis Rent A Car, our business is renting cars; our mission is total customer satisfaction.

Our goal is to provide the best quality customer service: to treat each customer the way we ourselves want to be treated. To exceed our customer's expectations.

We believe that only by maximizing our service and our productivity can we maximize our employee equity and our profits.

We are dedicated to a vigorous program of self-evaluation and improvement.

We continually strive to provide better and innovative services to enhance the travel experience for our customers. We work to strengthen our bonds with all active participants in the delivery of our service: our customers, our suppliers, and our co-workers in all areas.

We know that total customer service and satisfaction require the team effort of all employees, at all times.

"We try harder."

AVIS

Ethics

Ethics is a picture of what constitutes moral or immoral human conduct. What constitutes ethical or unethical behavior depends on our sense of meaning, our character, our habits, our virtues, and our personal values. Some have found ethical principles to be useful guidelines for sorting out differences between "right" and "wrong." Several examples are listed below:

Egoism: Promote the individual's best long-term interests.

Utilitarianism: Produce the greatest ratio of good to evil for everyone.

Golden Rule: Do unto others as you would have them do unto you.

Categorical Imperative: Behave in such a way that you wish the maxim of your action to be a universal law.[8]

The Moral Mission of Business

*T*he moral mission of business is to exercise all the imagination and initiative it can muster for the purpose of producing goods, services, and occasions for human achievement which make the world better.

THOMAS M. MULLIGAN[9]

Unfortunately, ethical principles are often rigid, inflexible, and difficult to apply. Take the Golden Rule, for example. Suppose a large American company is evaluating the pros and cons of building a huge lumbermill right in the middle of a Brazilian rain forest where human poverty is severe. One's perception of the effects of the mill is likely to be quite different depending on whether one views the problem from the perspective of an investor, a manager, a prospective employee, or a citizen with much environmental awareness. In this situation, the Golden Rule provides little guidance to management in reaching an ethical decision.

Were there any ethical principles at work in the story of the playhouse? If so, what were they? How were conflicts resolved?

A number of businesses, including Calvert Social Investment Fund, Eli Lilly, Tom's of Maine, and IBM have attempted to express their ethical principles and communicate them to their employees through a code of ethics. These codes vary in length from one-page summaries of several ethical principles to IBM's thirty-page "Business Conduct Guidelines," which treats topics ranging from protecting IBM's assets to fairness to competitors, bribery, gifts, business entertainment, conflict of interest, and antitrust laws.

Ethics Without the Sermon

1. Have you defined the problem accurately?
2. How would you define the problem if you stood on the other side of the fence?
3. How did this situation occur in the first place?
4. To whom and to what do you give your loyalty as a person and as a member of the corporation?
5. What is your intention in making the decision?
6. How does this intention compare with the probable results?
7. Whom could your decision or action injure?
8. Can you discuss the problem with the affected parties before you make your decision?
9. Are you confident that your position will be as valid over a long period of time as it seems now?
10. Could you disclose without qualm your decision or action to your boss, your CEO, the board of directors, your family, society as a whole?
11. What is the symbolic potential of your action if understood? If misunderstood?
12. Under what conditions would you allow exceptions to your stand?

LAURA NASH
Harvard Business Review[10]

The scandal at United Way has precipitated a closer examination of the ethical practices of many nonprofit organizations including child-sponsorship charities.[11] Seduced by emotionally charged television advertisements, hundreds of thousands of Americans send monthly checks to private child-sponsorship organizations like Childreach, Christian Children's Fund, Save the Children, and World Vision. The possibility of sponsoring one's own child in an impoverished third-world country has enormous appeal. It is neat, clean, tax-deductible, and hassle-free. You do not have to travel anywhere; you need not see or touch any smelly, filthy children; and you avoid the risk of disease and sickness. Even though you are completely detached from your child, writing a check makes you feel good.

But are these charitable organizations all they claim to be? How confident can you be that your contribution will actually benefit poor children?

The sad answer is that many child-sponsorship charities are not doing what they claim. That is in part because their governing boards are accountable to no one. In theory, trustees have a fiduciary responsibility for the donations collected to support needy children. However, government has few regulations to keep boards in line, and there are no stockholders to bring pressure to bear. Donors, charity staff members, and an organization's beneficiaries have no say in the election of the boards, which are usually self-perpetuating.

Unfortunately, when one joins the board of a large international charity, it is all too easy to be seduced by the "don't rock the boat" culture in which strategic planning, performance results, account-ability, and financial control are clearly secondary to organizational growth, public-relations gimmicks, and international razzmatazz. A press release announcing that a charity has received a $10,000 grant to provide relief to earthquake victims is far more important than evaluating whether the charity is equipped to handle the challenge of providing such assistance.

If individual board members are not paying attention to what is going on and are not doing their homework, a charity's managers are free to do whatever they choose. It is easy to distract the board with a discussion of which celebrity should appear in a charity's television spot—even though the board's time might be better spent figuring out whether the organization is carrying through on its promises to donors.

Board members who do a little digging will quickly find that not all charities are honest in their claims. Many child-sponsorship organizations, for example, tell prospective donors that eighty cents of every dollar they give will be used to benefit children and their families. That would be wonderful if it were true, but in reality, few charities have any idea what percentage of each sponsor's contributions actually reaches children. The financial- and management-control systems required to make such bold statements simply do not exist.

What's more, the audited financial reports of many of these organizations are misleading. The typical report contains no information about what is happening in particular countries or specific projects to help children. How much is actually being spent on overhead and fund-raising in a given country is completely unknown to the outside auditors, who are also unlikely to know whether funds may have been misappropriated through incompetence, fraud, or corruption. Monitoring child-assistance projects in developing nations is very difficult business.

Making matters worse is the enormous amount of record-keeping required to keep track of child-sponsorship activities. With one organization which one of us supported there was an accounting mix-up with every contribution made. A $500 gift to the charity's work in Guatemala resulted in three mutually contradictory thank-you notes, thus making me wonder what actually happened to the money I had contributed. In some cases, dead children end up getting sponsors.

Obeying the Law Is Not Enough

The law characteristically does not tell us what to do; rather, it tells us what *not* to do.

THOMAS H. MULLIGAN[12]

Another reason donors are often misled is that many charities play fast and loose in accounting for their in-kind donations. By acting as transfer agents that distribute large gifts of food, medicine, and medical supplies for needy nations, child-sponsorship organizations artificially inflate their incomes to counteract the effects of declining sponsorship revenues.

Because government agencies do so little to monitor charities, the task of policing the financial affairs of child-sponsorship organizations and other charities has been assumed by three private watchdog groups: the National Charities Information Bureau, the

Philanthropic Advisory Service of the Council of Better Business Bureaus, and the recently formed American Institute of Philanthropy.

What these watchdog groups have in common is that they publish evaluations of charities based almost entirely on information provided by the charities themselves. These toothless tigers possess neither the staff nor the resources to dig below the surface and investigate the efficiency of a charity's programs or whether it is upholding its pledges to donors.

Popular magazines like *Money,* in turn, process the information provided by the charities and the watchdog groups and publish their own rankings of charitable organizations. Many prospective donors incorrectly conclude that if a charity has been endorsed by a big-name magazine everything must be OK.

Child sponsorship is not just financially inefficient. Sponsored children are often viewed as superior to others, and the loss of sponsorship can be psychologically damaging.

Corporate Death Penalty

If a corporation . . . shows blatant disregard for the welfare of its customers, then its employees and/or the community at large should be able to petition to close down the company, causing its assets to be sold off . . . permanently dissolving the corporation. It is interesting to note that the death penalty for individuals is less controversial than the mere suggestion that a few corporations may have forfeited their right to exist. How many people does a company have to harm before we question if it ought to exist?

PAUL HAWKEN
The Ecology of Commerce [13]

The downsizing of corporate America provides dramatic evidence that growth for growth's sake is a mixed blessing—that bigger no longer means better. Just as many a corporate giant has become too big to manage effectively, so too have some global

child-sponsorship organizations and other large charities. The gap
between donors and beneficiaries is simply too great for there to
be any reasonable chance that projects will be effectively managed.
At one such organization, the fund-raising division attracts sponsors through advertising. An entirely different department man-
ages the sponsor relationships, and yet another sends the checks
from donors to the fund's offices abroad. Such overseas offices may
be responsible for more than one hundred projects in countries
like Brazil and India. Numerous layers of management are involved
in every program to help children abroad.

These problems are generic to most big international child-
sponsorship organizations and have little to do with the personali-
ties of individual managers. Horror stories abound, and they are
the logical consequences of too much money passing through too
many organizational levels to be of benefit to the children or their
sponsors.

The problems of the poor, the underprivileged, and the disfran-
chised are not responsive to solutions imposed by large hierarchical
organizations located thousands of miles away. To be truly effective,

---

A Code of Good Business Conduct

There are no alternatives to legal and ethical business
conduct. Individuals at every level of our organization
are personally responsible for their own business conduct. Anyone in doubt about the ethics or legality of
any action must consult with his or her principals' office
for a resolution of the question.

Federated as a company is totally committed to ethical
and legal behavior in every aspect of its business at
every level of the organization. Because we cannot possibly identify every ethical or legal question which might
arise in the course of our business, we must place the
burden of responsibility for scrupulous adherence to
ethical and legal practices on the individual.

FEDERATED DEPARTMENT STORES

---

antipoverty programs should be designed and implemented by people who live in a developing country or village. Ultimately, what we need is two-way dialogue between donors and the impoverished around the world. Unfortunately, that is a higher price than most of us are prepared to pay.

Statement of Corporate Responsibility

Given a set of values and ethical principles, how does one go about applying them to the various stakeholders of the company— investors, employees, managers, customers, distributors, suppliers, competitors, regulators, and society? That is precisely the aim of a statement of corporate responsibility. Such a statement attempts to sort out the relative priority which management assigns to each of the company's stakeholders.

Environmentally Friendly Business

Companies must re-envision and re-imagine them- selves as cyclical corporations, whose products either lit- erally disappear into harmless components, or whose products are so specific and targeted to a specific func- tion that there is no spillover effect, no waste, no ran- dom molecules dancing in the cells of wildlife; in other words, no forms of life must be adversely affected.

PAUL HAWKEN
The Ecology of Commerce [14]

In an attempt to please everyone, all too many statements of corporate responsibility turn out to be bland statements about apple pie, motherhood, and the American flag. If a statement of corporate responsibility is to have any real bite, it must state whether employees, customers, or investors are more important. The entire credibility of the management philosophy will be un- dermined if the philosophy says one thing but managerial behavior is always antithetical to the stated philosophy. The philosophy

Gardener's Supply Company

OUR VISION
Solutions for a Living Earth

We envision a world in harmony with nature, where the rewards of successful gardening are available to all. We will pursue this vision by building a successful, gardening-related business dedicated to the long-term well-being of our employees, our customers, and our Planet.

OUR MISSION
Business That Makes a Difference

We provide innovative gardening-related products, services, and information of the highest possible quality and best value. We do this by understanding and solving the challenges faced by our gardening customers.

We care about our customers and we make customer satisfaction our top priority, reflecting this in all marketing, product, and operations activities and decisions.

Recognizing that individual responsibility and enthusiasm are critical to our success, we make *the creation of an alive and supportive corporate culture* an equally high priority. We care about our employees and use an open and participatory management style to involve them in bringing meaning and pleasure to the workplace.

We operate our business to *achieve profitable growth* as a means to increase value for our shareholders, and to create opportunities and increase financial rewards for our employees. We believe long-term financial success is best achieved if we act honestly and fairly.

should not make gratuitous statements about the importance of customers and employees unless management is prepared to act accordingly.

Since Morfar and his grandsons are the owners, investors, employees, and consumers of the Swedish playhouse, problems of social responsibility are somewhat simplified. But is that not an important lesson from the story?

Love Canal, the Exxon *Valdez*, Three Mile Island, Bhopal, the Dalkon Shield, and defense contractors who supply weapons to Third World dictators have made some individual and institutional investors uncomfortable with investments in companies whose business practices are socially irresponsible. To meet the needs of more socially minded investors, a number of self-described socially responsible mutual funds such as the Pax World Fund and the Calvert Social Investment Fund have emerged. Every potential investment is first screened for financial soundness then evaluated according to a specific set of social criteria.

Portfolio Social Criteria

The Fund seeks investments in companies that are not to any degree engaged in manufacturing defense or weapons-related products. The Fund excludes from its portfolio securities of companies: (1) engaged in military activities, defined as follows: (a) appearing on the Department of Defense's 100 largest contractors list and (b) other companies contracting with the Department of Defense if 5% or more of their gross sales were derived from such contracts; (2) engaged in liquor, tobacco, and gambling industries. In addition, the Fund will seek out companies with fair employment and pollution control policies and practices, and invest in some international development.

PAX WORLD FUND

Reality Check

Many of the statements of management philosophy presented in this chapter are very appealing. Most have a nice ring to them. But are they consistent with the real-world environments in which some of these companies operate? Let's have a closer look.

For example, is it really possible for a company like Publix to treat its customers, employees, managers, suppliers, and shareholders as well as the company's statement of management philosophy suggests? It all seems a bit idealistic.

Was IBM's policy of laying off 200,000 employees in the early 1990s consistent with its professed belief in "respect for the individual"? There were more humane options available including executive salary reductions, shorter working hours, and job sharing. How much respect is expressed for an individual who is let go even though he or she is doing a good job?

Should Avis' customers be made aware of the fact that General Motors owns more than one fourth of the equity in Avis? No mention is made in the code of conduct of Federated Department Stores of the ethics of promoting consumerism and a lifestyle based on having. Is Gardener's Supply's policy of sending out millions of catalogs each year consistent with "a world in harmony with nature"? Why is it so difficult to have one's name removed from their mailing list?

These are but a few of the questions raised by some of these statements of management philosophy. If a company publishes a code of conduct or management philosophy, it should be prepared for the inevitable heat, justifiable or not, generated by skeptical employees, investors, and customers.

Writing an honest, coherent management philosophy is by no means an easy task. Balancing the conflicting interests of owners, managers, employees, and customers requires considerable skill. No formal management philosophy at all may be better than one which deliberately tries to mislead.

Chapter 6

SELF-EMPLOYMENT

Man does not suffer so much from poverty today as he suffers from the fact that he has become a cog in a large machine, an automaton, that his life has become empty and lost its meaning.

ERICH FROMM
ESCAPE FROM FREEDOM[1]

Finding Meaningful Employment

From our analysis of the quest for meaning in the workplace, two conclusions emerge. First, finding meaningful work is a difficult undertaking. Second, creating a work environment which will facilitate employees' search for meaning is equally challenging. Little Max and Lucas found meaningful work in Sweden, but what about Mike the American steelworker?

Whether one is searching for meaningful employment or attempting to fashion a work environment that will enhance the meaningfulness of employees' work, the answers to seven questions are of fundamental importance:

1. Who is doing the work?
2. How is the work organized?
3. What is the nature of the work?
4. What is the product of the work?
5. Who benefits from the product?
6. Who may be harmed by the production or consumption of the product?
7. How are employees compensated?

If we believe that the search for meaning is somehow connected to the care and nurturing of our soul, then how can we take charge

Nice Work If You Can Get It

The type of work which modern technology is most successful in reducing or even eliminating is skillful, productive work of human hands, in touch with real materials of one kind or another. In an advanced industrial society, such work has become exceedingly rare, and to make a decent living by doing such work has become virtually impossible. A great part of the modern neurosis may be due to this very fact; for the human being, defined by Thomas Aquinas as a being with brains and hands, enjoys nothing more than to be creatively, usefully, productively engaged with both his hands and his brains. Today, a person has to be wealthy to be able to enjoy this simple thing, this very great luxury: he has to be able to afford space and good tools; he has to be lucky enough to find a good teacher and plenty of free time to learn and practice. He really has to be rich enough not to need a job; for the number of jobs that would be satisfactory in these respects is very small indeed.

E. F. Schumacher
Small Is Beautiful[2]

of our soul, if we are marching to the beat of another drummer who tells us what to do, how to do it, and when to do it? No matter what kind of business one may be in, there are endless possibilities for conflict and tension between those who actually do the work and those who manage the enterprise. It is very difficult to be your own boss—to be a free person—if you owe your soul to the company store.

In no sense are we arguing that self-employment is the only means by which one can find meaning in the workplace. Yet in our complex, highly interdependent industrial economy, finding meaning in large organizations, whether they be business, government, or nonprofit enterprises, is not an easy task. No matter what

> ### Doing Your Own Thing
>
> Not to take possession of your life plan is to let your existence be an accident.
>
> IRVIN D. YALOM
> *When Nietzsche Wept*[3]

the product may be, multilayered bureaucratic organizations tend to stifle one's search for meaning. If we feel we have no control over our own destiny in a large enterprise, then we may soon become disillusioned and alienated. If employees possess no stake in the enterprise—economically or psychologically—then sustained meaningfulness is impossible to achieve. From an organizational standpoint, employee participation and ownership are of critical importance to the search for meaning in the workplace. Some companies attempt to simulate the benefits of self-employment and employee ownership through communitarian management practices.

Obviously the nature of one's work itself is an important determinant of meaning. Mindless, boring, repetitive clerical or assembly-line jobs do little to enhance one's quest for meaning at work. Consider as examples Dr. Scrooge and Dr. Goodwill, both of whom engage in highly repetitive professional work. Dr. Scrooge is an endodontist specializing in root canal therapy. One of us had the misfortune of being his patient.

I arrived on time for a 1:00 P.M. appointment with Dr. Scrooge. Thirty minutes later, his receptionist had not even acknowledged my presence in the waiting room. At 1:45, forty-five minutes late, the receptionist told me Dr. Scrooge was ready to see me. No mention was made of the delay. Without any explanation of what was involved in having three simultaneous root canals, he proceeded to anesthetize my gums in preparation for the procedure. During the entire hour-and-a-half process, Dr. Scrooge said not one word to me. He did not feel obligated to inform me that the roots of one of my teeth had died and could cause complications. When the procedure was completed, his receptionist handed me a bill for $1,200, which I was expected to pay before leaving the office. Two days later infection had set in where the roots had died, and I suffered excruciating pain. Dr. Scrooge's nurse gave me some antibiotics and seemed surprised that I had not been warned of the likely side effects of the root canal procedure.

Dr. Scrooge is a money-making machine, and I was just another nameless patient. He made no attempt whatsoever to connect with me as a human being. He appeared to be extremely bored with his work and completely alienated from his receptionist, nurse, and patients.

Dr. Goodwill, an ophthalmologist, has been conducting routine eye examinations four days a week for more than twenty-five years. An eye examination is a highly repetitive mechanistic procedure. Dr. Goodwill has done so many eye examinations he can no doubt do one with his eyes closed. He never makes a mistake. I often thought when I visited him, "How could someone as intelligent and well-educated as he tolerate the repetitive nature of this boring work?" But on several occasions I sat right outside his office and listened to him as he interacted with each patient ahead of me. Without exception, whether the patient was rich or poor, black or white, Dr. Goodwill was completely engaged with each patient as a separate and distinct human being. He was connected with each of his patients. It was a pleasure to experience his humanness.

Thus we have two sophisticated health-care professionals engaged in quite repetitive work—one finds his work painfully boring and almost meaningless, the other is engaged in a meaningful way with each and every patient.

Whether one's work is meaningful or not may also depend on the nature of the fruits of one's labor. If someone is trying to find meaning from being, then it's hard to imagine that working for a company which produces low-quality plastic toys and consumer goods could ever prove to be very meaningful. On the other hand, some people might find meaning producing life-saving pharmaceutical products regardless of how boring the work might be. For those who reject nihilism, handgun and automatic assault weapon production must seem meaningless. Companies that ignore the environmental consequences of their actions are flirting with nihilism.

The Doughnut Principle

The doughnut principle suggests that if you cannot get existential development [meaning] from your current job, you should either change jobs or make sure that the empty spaces in your personal doughnut are filled somewhere else. One job does not have to fill all needs.

CHARLES HANDY
The Age of Paradox [4]

There are also those who find meaning in their work only because it enables them to do something else which is meaningful to them. For example, it is not uncommon to find artists, writers, and musicians who teach in schools or colleges primarily to support their art, writing, and music respectively. Many journalists write for newspapers so they can afford to write novels, short stories, or poetry. For some people, their work is just a "hobby" which affords them the opportunity to do their real hobby which is their true vocation.

How and by whom one is compensated for one's services may also influence the meaningfulness of one's work. Consider, for example, the practice of medicine. In most countries physicians are paid a salary. In the United States physicians who are in private practice make more money if their patients are very sick and remain in the hospital for long periods of time. The practice of medicine in our country is primarily a business. For the physician, does meaning stem from the service provided to patients or from the money received from them?

We believe that meaning can be found by virtually anyone whether one be a believer or a nonbeliever, rich or poor, young or old, educated or uneducated. There are many paths to meaning in the workplace, but few, if any, avoid confronting our human need for love and empathy and our intense longing for connectedness. Most combine a journey inward with an outward quest. We now turn our attention to self-employment—the first of five strategies for meaningful work to be considered.

Five Strategies for Meaningful Work

1. *Self-Employment*—do your own thing.
2. *Employee Ownership*—go to work for an employee-owned company like UPS or Avis.
3. *Participatory Management*—seek employment with an organization that is into power sharing, tension reduction, and other communitarian management practices.
4. *Value-Based Management*—join a firm that combines social responsibility with profitability.
5. *Reinventing Work*—participate in the creation of a work environment based on being rather than having.

Escape from Corporate America

It is hardly surprising that more than three-fourths of the American workforce is employed by private business. Since the end of World War II, American corporations—particularly large corporations—have provided their employees with job security, increased income, social status, health insurance, and other fringe benefits. In return employees have been expected to forgo most of the rights usually associated with a free society—freedom of assembly, freedom of expression, and due process. For an elite corps of corporate managers, playing the corporate game—and winning—not only provides meaning to their lives but high adventure as well. These corporate elites have no problem playing by a set of rules they created, since they are the primary beneficiaries of the rules. And yet there is a price to be paid for this access to the benefit stream of large corporations: corporate loyalty and unremitting conformity. A good corporate citizen is one who is always agreeable and abides by the rules. Dissent is not perceived as a virtue in the corporate executive suite.

Human Scale

*T*here must be an alternative to nations grown too big, to governments grown too dangerous, to bureaucracies grown too inflated, to systems grown too complex, to enterprises grown too unwieldy, to corporations grown too immense, to production grown too massive, to cities grown too crowded, to buildings grown too vast, to tools grown too complicated, to relations grown too distended.

There is: human scale.

KIRKPATRICK SALE
Human Scale [5]

Strange though it may seem, there are millions of American workers who not only don't object to being told what to do, they seem to prefer it that way. There are numerous examples of employees being offered increased opportunities to participate in managerial decision making only to refuse to accept the additional responsibility.

At least one explanation for this type of behavior lies in the fact that some people may actually prefer a mindless, less demanding job with few decisions so they will have the energy and the time to be with their families and enjoy their time away from work even more. A mindless job may also help keep work in perspective.

Obeying Others

*H*e who does not obey himself is ruled by others. It is easier, far easier, to obey another than to command yourself.

IRVIN D. YALOM
When Nietzsche Wept [6]

Executive MBA's working full-time for corporations fantasize about the possibility of escaping from the corporate rat race and starting their own business. Few of them ever do so. Until very recently, the economic power of Corporate America has proved to be very seductive. However, corporate restructuring, downsizing, and the layoff of tens of millions of employees have tarnished the image of some large corporations like AT&T, IBM, and Delta Air Lines. Less job security, reduced fringe benefits, and tougher work rules are all part of the new "lean and mean" corporation. With the increased use of temporary employees, companies try to avoid paying any fringe benefits whatsoever. Many former corporate managers have literally been forced into self-employment for the sake of economic survival.[7]

Ironically, while millions are being forced out of Corporate America because of restructuring and downsizing, the rapidly deteriorating situation in the American health-care industry has forced droves of private physicians either out of business or into the arms of Corporate America. Because of previous abuses among private physicians, hospitals, and insurance companies, the entire health-care system is becoming more centralized, forcing private physicians into H.M.O.'s (Health Maintenance Organizations) and other large managed-care networks. The self-employed, solo-practice physician may soon cease to exist. At least in the short run, the entire health-care field seems to be headed toward even bigger clinics, hospitals, insurance companies, and drug companies. The personal touch of the friendly, family, neighborhood physician has been replaced by the large, bureaucratic H.M.O. and megahospital. Medicine is no longer a healing art, but rather a very big impersonal business. How long will it take the public to discover that big corporate medicine is not necessarily better medicine?

Craftsmanship

Craftsmanship is an important source of self-employment in the Green Mountains of Vermont. Hans is an Austrian American craftsman, someone who knows from years of experience, trial and error, testing and learning, how to work with wood in Vermont's

Northeast Kingdom. He stands looking at a pile of wood, sizing it up, surveying it carefully. Then he thrusts his hand into the stack of boards, grasping one and removing it. He turns the board over, rubs his hand along the edges, rejects it, and draws forth another. He repeats this exercise with a dozen or so boards. The pieces of wood are touched, turned over, sized up, and rejected. He even smells them. At last one is judged to be right.

In an age of plastic, stamped out, mass-produced everything, it is a joy to meet someone who has those skills which take time and patience to acquire, standards of judgment and expertise which cannot be bought. Hans's life is obviously better, richer, more interesting because of his craft, and the lives of others have been enriched by his craftsmanship as well. We all seem to possess a great need and a great ability to create. Rarely are we content to leave the world as we have found it. Max and Lucas discovered this at an early age while working on their playhouse.

Craftsmanship

There is no ulterior motive in work other than the product being made and the processes of its creation. The details of daily work are meaningful because they are not detached in the worker's mind from the product of the work. The worker is free to control his own working action. The craftsman is thus able to learn from his work; and to use and develop his capacities and skills in its prosecution. There is no split of work and play, or work or culture. The craftsman's way of livelihood determines and infuses his entire mode of living.

C. W. MILLS
White Collar [8]

To carve a wooden animal, build a sailboat, plant a garden, prepare a gourmet meal, rebuild an old Thunderbird, or construct a cathedral—we are often most alive, most ourselves when we are engaged in some act of creativity. Creativity transforms us from detached observers of life into responsible participants.

The Bible on Creativity

*T*hen God said, "Let us make humankind in our image, according to our likeness; and let them have dominion."

So God created humankind in his image, . . . male and female he created them.

God blessed them, and God said to them, "Be fruitful and multiply, and fill the earth and subdue it."

God saw everything that he had made, and indeed, it was very good.

(GEN. 1:26, 27-28, 31)

Creativity is more than simply adding objects to our world (another form of having). From what we have observed, the act of creation is of more consequence in our search for meaning than the thing created. Creativity is not simply throwing blobs of paint on a canvas, spontaneous outbursts of energy channeled into painting or poetry or wood. Creation involves engagement, discipline, learning skills, mastering technique.

Consider the many creative skills of former *Business Week* writer Reggi Ann Dubin, who from her mountaintop home in Chittenden, Vermont, writes all the speeches of American Airlines chairperson Robert L. Crandall and operates a highly successful business, Chittenden Kitchens. Whenever Crandall needs to deliver a speech, Reggi spends hours in her high-tech home office crafting every word of her high-profile client's next address. When she's not speechwriting, Reggi is supervising the production and marketing of thousands of jars of a sinfully delicious cranberry sauce known as Cranberrie Yummie.

Cranberrie Yummie, and its kindred products Cranberrie Rummie and Cranberrie Hunnie, is no ordinary cranberry sauce. It is produced from cranberries and a secret combination of spices and herbs carefully selected by Reggi. She and five neighbors cook the exotic sauce on their own stoves. The ability to select the proper cranberries, herbs, and spices; to know how to control the stove; and how long to cook the sauce are not natural abilities. One must have experienced many New England Thanksgiving and Christmas turkey dinners to be able to produce such a sophisticated taste treat as Cranberrie Yummie.

We live in an age of instant gratification, where people are deceived into thinking that they can buy French food out of a box and serve it up instantly from the microwave. Yet in our better moments we know that good things in life take time—that few worthwhile things are had without effort, without the disciplined submission to the skills and virtues of a craft. Surely the widespread interest in gourmet cooking, arts and crafts, sewing and handiwork, is due to many people's realization that we are at our best when we are creating—when we are consciously engaged with the world around us. As we have seen, many modern jobs are dull, repetitious, uncreative. Our schools continue to crank out students who are adept at spitting back facts and figures on exams and inept at cooking a good meal or making a table, much less playing the violin. Too often, as children, our experiences with art or music, with crafts or creative writing have served only to convince us that we are not creative, that we can never master the skills required to contribute beauty or pleasure to the world. That means, for many of us, adulthood must be a time for acquiring those skills and disciplines, freedom and confidence necessary to create.

Our creations remind us that we ought not to over-intellectualize the search for meaning. For most of us, meaning is not found exclusively in books. Few of us live by noble ideas. Rather, we receive meaning from our creations and from the very act of creation.

So stimulating emotionally, spiritually, and intellectually is the monthly piano lesson of Alexander Naylor with master Suzuki teacher Robert Fraley, that his parents hardly mind at all the two-hour drive to the quaint garage-top studio in New London, New

Hampshire. As one catches a first glimpse of the two grand pianos situated on the second floor of Fraley's green garage, one gains the distinct impression that a piano lesson with Mr. Fraley is going to be very serious business. It is, but it is also fun!

A music lesson with Robert Fraley is not only an adventure in creativity but a lesson in music history, music philosophy, and theology combined into one two-hour session. With his tales of classical composers, the history of jazz, and personal anecdotes, his students come away highly motivated and energized. Fraley's message is the same whether it be aimed at a handicapped three-year-old or a ninety-year-old grandmother: "Playing the piano is fun." With his warm, self-confident style, his delightful sense of humor, and his complete professionalism, Fraley fills his students with love, an appreciation of good music, and a commitment to hard work. His students learn to play good music by first listening to good music.

Robert Fraley is a person who derives meaning not only from his own music but from his students and their music as well. Music is Mr. Fraley's life.

Artistic Encouragement

*P*raise must be used judiciously and honestly. Praise implies an external reward and thus suggests competition. Instead of praise, substitute encouragement. Honest praise cannot be given unless the student has improved, but encouragement is all-embracing. Encouragement is long-range and helps the student to have self-respect and self-confidence. Teachers should always treasure their students' efforts rather than their accomplishments. Instead of saying, "Oh, that was very good! But . . ." say, "I have faith in you. You're doing fine."

ROBERT FRALEY
New London, New Hampshire

The Family Farm

Another important form of self-employment is the family farm. While the sixty-year exodus of small farmers to American cities continues, the family farm remains a cherished tradition in Western Europe. The European Union supports ten times the number of farmers found in our country. Unlike their counterparts in the United States, small farms are still a valued way of life in Europe. In some years, as many as 100,000 family farms have gone out of business in the United States. Reflecting the low priority Americans place on the family farm, traditional farming is being devoured and replaced by huge corporate-owned megafarms. More than half the food in America is now produced by only 4 percent of our farms. Corporate farms increasingly depend on chemicals, pesticides, and energy-guzzling methods of raising crops and transporting them long distances to market. Corporate farmers are obsessed with high crop yields, which destroy rather than nurture the soil. As family farms fade away, so too do rural communities including businesses, schools, and hospitals.

Family Farming

*W*e believe the survival of the family farm is crucial to all of us. It's the historic, living foundation of our food supply, our values, and the rural communities from which our country has always drawn strength, character and economic security.

BEN & JERRY'S

African Americans in particular were not motivated to remain on the exploitative tenant farms to which they were relegated after the Civil War. Anything Chicago, Cleveland, or Detroit had to offer was better than life in the Mississippi Delta. The quality of education, medical care, cultural life, transportation, and public utilities available throughout rural America in the 1940s and 1950s provided little incentive for white farmers to remain in the countryside either. There was an arrogant attitude among our increasingly urban population that life on the farm was not worth preserving. We have paid dearly for our myopic views and policies toward rural America. Many of our worst urban social and economic problems are directly attributable to our inability to create a more balanced approach to urban and rural development since World War II.

The Urban-Rural Imbalance

The all-pervading disease of the modern world is the total imbalance between city and countryside, an imbalance in terms of wealth, power, culture, attraction, and hope. The former has become over-extended and the latter has atrophied. The city has become the universal magnet, while rural life has lost its savor. Yet it remains an unalterable truth that, just as a sound mind depends on a sound body, so the health of the cities depends on the health of the rural areas. The cities, with all their wealth, are merely secondary producers, while primary production, the precondition of all economic life, takes place in the countryside. The prevailing lack of balance, based on the age-old exploitation of countryman and raw material producer, today threatens all countries throughout the world, the rich even more than the poor. To restore a proper balance between city and rural life is perhaps the greatest task in front of modern man. It is not simply a matter of raising agricultural yields so as to avoid world hunger. There is no answer to the evils of mass unemployment and mass migration into cities, unless the whole level of rural life can be raised, and this requires the development of an agro-industrial culture, so that each district, each community, can offer a colorful variety of occupations to its members.

E. F. SCHUMACHER
Small Is Beautiful[9]

Unlike United States policy, agricultural subsidies in Europe have been designed to protect small farmers. Although European farms are much smaller and less efficient than American farms and food costs are higher, there are many compensating benefits. Since small European farms use fewer nitrates, pesticides, and herbicides, wells and streams are much less likely to be contaminated than in the United States. Because the quality of life has remained high in small European towns and villages, one does not find the urban poverty, crime, hopelessness, and despair in European cities which can be found in New York, Washington, Los Angeles, and Detroit.

Functions of Agriculture

To keep in touch with living nature, of which one is and remains a highly vulnerable part.

To humanize and ennoble one's wider habitat.

To bring forth the food stuffs and other materials which are needed for a becoming life.

E. F. SCHUMACHER
Small Is Beautiful[10]

What we have managed to do in this country over the past half-century is transfer the alienation, poverty, and despair of the small family farmer from the countryside to the inner-city ghettos of our large metropolitan areas. Even though farming ranks only third, behind manufacturing and tourism, as a source of state income, the family farm is still the heart and soul of tiny Vermont. When compared with the other forty-nine states, Vermont is small, rural (67.8 percent), democratic, egalitarian, and not violent. The moral fabric of the state has been strongly influenced by Vermont family farmers. Vermont values like resourcefulness, hard work, education, versatility, and inventiveness can be traced directly to the family farm. According to a very popular myth, not so many years ago there were more black-and-white Holsteins, Brown Swiss, and Guernseys in Vermont than there were people. Although the myth turns out to be just that—a myth—many Vermonters wish that it were true. Today there are fewer than 7,000 farms in Vermont of which fewer than 2,000 are dairy farms. In 1950 there were more than 11,000 dairy farms alone, but reduced government milk subsidies, oversupply, and the rising cost of technology have driven thousands of Vermont farmers off the land. Dairy products still account for three-fourths of agricultural income, but cattle, vegetables, apples, hay, and maple syrup are also important cash crops. The average farm size in Vermont is only 219 acres, compared with the national average of 468 acres.

The Vermont Farmer

For all Vermonters it is the farmer who produces closest to the land. Historically, during the centuries when agricultural life gave form and substance to Vermont, the farmer was not a party to the manipulation of paper values and the realization of windfall gains, or to a life without hard physical work in such conditions as the changing seasons would provide. His was the world of the genuine, the natural, the God-given. He arose before dawn, conformable to the needs of his livestock. He savored the pungent aroma of the cow barn, the fragrance of the apple blossoms in May, the smell of the new-mown hay. He and his farm wife planned their life together to do what had to be done, cutting wood for the winter and the sugaring, fixing fence, seeing the milk safely to the dairy, guiding their son's hands for the first time he steered team or tractor, putting up food for the long winters. Affluent the farmer was not, but strong in mind and spirit, an essential working part of a beautiful though sometimes severe world which made sense—and was profoundly satisfying—to those who dwelt within it.

FRANK BRYAN AND JOHN MCCLAUGHRY
The Vermont Papers[11]

Although the backwoods isolation of Vermont's hills and valleys fosters self-sufficiency, it also provides a breeding ground for real community seldom found in America. From the outset, the combination of the harsh winters and the small farms, villages, and towns has engendered a variety of communal activities including barn-raising, work bees, electric co-ops, and—more recently—cohousing, communal farming, and intentional communities.

Doing Your Own Thing

The Internal Revenue Service estimates that roughly fifteen million Americans—13 percent of the workforce—are primarily self-employed. This figure does not include small farmers and tens of thousands of self-employed people working in the underground economy who report nothing to the I.R.S.

Although the group includes physicians, dentists, artists, writers, plumbers, and others who have traditionally worked for themselves, more than four million have been forced into self-employment as a result of corporate downsizing, mergers, layoffs, budget cuts, and a weak American economy.[12] The ranks of this latter group swelled by 700,000 during the decade of the 1980s. Many of the newly self-employed are highly skilled managers and professionals who have been laid off by large corporations. They are now "independent consultants" working much harder than in the past and at a fraction of their previous salary. They have discovered that although it is far easier to start your own business in the United States than in most countries, making a living this way is not nearly so easy.

It is estimated that nearly fifty million people now work either part-time or full-time in their homes as telecommuters, moonlighters, or business owners. As a result of downsizing and corporate restructuring, many companies now hire a significant number of temporary employees, independent consultants, and freelances to do the work previously done by in-house personnel. Personal computer technology has further reinforced this trend. Thousands of individuals are now employed in their homes as independent accountants, financial advisors, travel agents, market researchers, word processors, computer programmers, design engineers, writers, and public relations specialists. We seem to be experiencing a veritable explosion in self-employment in the home.

The modern label for this new type of cottage industry is *outsourcing*. Outsourcing enables employers to cut costs and to be more flexible in responding to rapidly changing business conditions. The tools of this emerging new trade are the home computer, the car telephone, and the fax machine. The benefits of this form of self-employment to independent contractors are obvious: flexibility, low overhead, self-actualization, and the chance to be one's own boss. Husbands and wives can share child-care and homemaking responsibilities in this type of work environment.

Although outsourcing has created a substantial number of new opportunities for meaningful work, it is not without some serious risks. It is quite possible for these independent operators to end up with no health insurance, few training opportunities, and very limited job security.

To determine whether or not you are suited for working at home, you may want to ask yourself the following questions:

1. Do you like working alone?
2. Are you well-disciplined?
3. Is your work-space adequate?
4. Do you have the proper equipment?
5. Can you afford to live on an irregular income?
6. Do you have access to health insurance?
7. Do you possess the necessary business skills?
8. Are there any residential zoning problems?
9. Do you have adequate working space for clients?
10. Will your work be disturbed by noisy children or neighbors?

Corporate America:
Through a Different Looking Glass

For millions of American working people, Corporate America, large nonprofit organizations, and big government bureaucracies are perceived to be the only game in town in terms of suitable employment opportunities. How is it possible to cope in such large monolithic organizations without giving up one's freedom and personal integrity?

Clearly there are no easy answers to this troubling question. But if one hopes to survive in such a regimented environment without losing one's sanity and integrity, then one must give considerable thought to the answers for the following questions:

1. Who am I?
2. Why am I here?
3. Where am I going?
4. What is the purpose of my life?

Unless one has a firm sense of grounding, it is all too easy to be wheeled and spun by one's boss, one's peers, the marketplace, government regulations, or social mores. To maintain one's sense of balance in a large organization, one must have a clear picture of one's personal sense of meaning, values, ethics, and sense of social responsibility. Otherwise a new boss, a promotion opportunity, or a change in corporate policy can leave one reeling without any sense of direction whatsoever.

What price are you willing to pay for a salary increase or a promotion? Are you willing to stretch the truth a little to make a sale or obtain a big contract? If your boss asks you to do something you consider to be unethical, what will you do? Will you confront your boss? Will you resign? Will you blow the whistle?

How much responsibility will you assume for undemocratic, unethical, or socially irresponsible business practices? Will you pass the buck? Blame top management? Or step forward and accept your share of the blame?

Many managers and employees fail to realize that they often have much more freedom and indeed more power than they may have initially perceived. The real question is, How do you use your freedom and your power?

In the next four chapters we consider the question of how one might emulate a self-employment environment even in a large organization. Of particular interest is whether or not elements of the Swedish playhouse story can be replicated in the real world.

Chapter 7

EMPLOYEE OWNERSHIP

There is no bigger incentive than for someone to work for himself. . . . The basic principle which I believe has contributed to the building of our business as it exists today is the ownership of our company by the people employed by it.

JAMES E. CASEY, FOUNDER
UNITED PARCEL SERVICE

If one is either unable or unwilling to start one's own business, then going to work for an employee-owned business may provide a second-best alternative—an alternative which seems to be increasing in popularity in the United States these days. More than fourteen million employees in nearly 10,000 enterprises now own a stake in the company for which they work, the best known of which are Avis, Kroger, McDonnell Douglas, Rockwell International, United Airlines, and United Parcel Service. However, employees own a majority of the stock in only about a quarter of these companies. We shall concentrate exclusively on those employee-owned companies in which a majority of the shares are owned by the employees.

Throughout the Cold War many Americans were skeptical of employee ownership, since it was equated with socialism, which had strong negative connotations in an intolerant, strongly anti-Communist environment. In reality, work cooperation in America originated not with Soviet and Eastern European Communists but rather with Native Americans hundreds of years ago. The political, economic, and social practices of a number of tribes—most notably the Iroquois—were highly communal in nature. The concept of private ownership of land was unknown to the ten thousand Iroquois in the early seventeenth century. All forms of work were done cooperatively including hunting, farming, and food preparation. Food, housing, and tools were shared within the communal group.

Employee-owned enterprises are usually organized either as *work cooperatives* or as *employee stock ownership plans* (E.S.O.P.s). Ownership and control of worker cooperatives resides in the membership, where each worker has one equal vote. Unlike conventional for-profit corporations, stockholder (member) dividends are taxed only once. A cooperative does not pay income taxes on that portion of its profits that is distributed to members as dividends. E.S.O.P.s are enterprises in which employees may buy stock through payroll deductions. They provide a number of substantial tax benefits to employees and outside financiers to encourage employee ownership. Whether a particular employee-owned enterprise is organized as a worker cooperative or as an E.S.O.P. usually depends on the financial situation of the company and the tax laws of the state where it was organized.

Employee-owned enterprises range in size from United Parcel with annual revenues in excess of $20 billion and more than 300,000 employees to tiny Vermont-based Cherry Hill Cannery, which has only a handful of worker-owners. In worker cooperatives and democratically organized E.S.O.P.s, those who do the work decide what the company produces, how the work is done, and how the profits are distributed. Ideally, these enterprises embody the following principles:

1. employee democracy
2. worker-member equality
3. equitable profit sharing
4. voluntary, nondiscriminatory employment
5. open records and meetings
6. limited return on capital
7. required workers' consent to sell the business[1]

Among the benefits of worker cooperatives and E.S.O.P.s cited by Krimerman and Lindenfeld in their book *When Workers Decide* are bottom-up control; improved self-respect, happiness, and personal growth; wage security; job creation and preservation; and community orientation.[2]

United Parcel Service

Not only is United Parcel Service the largest, best-known, and most successful employee-owned company in America, but it is the world's largest parcel carrier, carrying more than three billion parcels annually in 185 countries throughout North America, South America, Europe, and Asia. UPS operates more than 120,000 vehicles (package cars, vans, tractors, trailers), owns 220 jet aircraft, and leases another 300 planes.

Known for the reliability of its service and its low-cost rates, UPS is by far the most profitable transportation company in the United States. Its founder, James E. Casey, declared that the company must be "owned by its managers and managed by its owners." Although UPS is probably not the most democratic of the employee-owned companies in America, it still works very well. It is owned entirely by 26,000 of its managers and supervisors. Through a generous annual bonus plan and an employee stock option plan, some employees who began their careers as UPS clerks and drivers have retired as multimillionaires.

As evidence that UPS works, how many times have you ever seen a UPS delivery person walk to your front door with a parcel? Most of the time the men and women who drive the distinctive dark-olive trucks literally run to your front door. Employee turnover rates at UPS are among the lowest in the nation.

Publix Supermarkets

Ranked among the top ten companies in America for which to work, Florida-based Publix Supermarkets with sales in excess of $8 billion and more than 90,000 employees is the second largest entirely employee-owned company in the United States. Known for its immaculate stores, high quality, superior customer service, state-of-the-art technology, and fast checkout, Publix operates 415 supermarkets in Florida and a handful in Georgia and South Carolina.

Publix

*M*uch of our society keeps moving toward the depersonalized, toward making people feel like numbers. It has been a real privilege to see a large and growing business reverse this trend, a business that honors its employees and has become fabulously successful in the process.

DANIEL YANKELOVICH
Market Researcher

Unlike UPS, whose shareholders are restricted to managers and supervisors, any part-time or full-time employee of Publix who has worked for the company for one year can purchase shares. There are 57,500 Publix shareholders, all of whom are either employees or former employees. Nonemployees cannot purchase Publix shares. By comparison with other supermarket chains, Publix's employees—called associates—enjoy higher wages, better fringe benefits, profit sharing, annual bonuses, and promotion from within.

The company's internal promotion policy has created an environment where even the most high-ranking officers know firsthand about mopping floors and stocking the shelves. Regional vice presidents participate in training new associates, serving as role models for the promotion-from-within philosophy which results in a cohesive, highly motivated workforce. Not unlike their UPS counterparts, some bagclerks who became Publix managers have retired as wealthy individuals.

Publix Guarantee

*W*e will never, knowingly, disappoint you. If for any reason your purchase does not give you complete satisfaction, the full purchase price will be cheerfully refunded immediately upon request. We have always believed no sale is complete until the meal is eaten and enjoyed.

GEORGE W. JENKINS, FOUNDER

However, in spite of its many virtues, Publix has not been able to rid itself of widespread nepotism and paternalism. Its chairperson and CEO Howard Jenkins is the son of the company's founder, George Jenkins. Four other relatives of the founder sit on the company's board of directors. According to public relations manager Bob McDermott, "Nepotism is the heartbeat of our company. We have cashiers with husbands who are truck drivers and executives whose wives are cashiers. It is all through the ranks, and we are proud of it. It provides a good comfort zone because we know who we are working with." The tight-knit family atmosphere and good-old-boy network at Publix have made it tough for minorities and women to get into management.

United Airlines

In July 1994, after seven years of negotiations, one of the longest-running buyout efforts in history was concluded resulting in the employees of United Airlines acquiring a 55 percent ownership stake in the company in exchange for wage and work-rule concessions valued at $4.9 billion over six years. About 54,000 of the airline's 75,500 employees were involved in the buyout and took immediate pay cuts. This marks the first time a relatively healthy airline has given its employees control in exchange for wage rollbacks. In the early 1980s, ailing Pan Am, Eastern, Western, and Republic offered their employees ownership in return for work concessions. In the case of Pan Am and Eastern, which were in dire straits, it was too little, too late. Western and Republic were subsequently acquired by stronger carriers. T.W.A., U.S. Air, and Northwest have offered their employees ownership, but not control. United is now the third largest employee-controlled company in the United States.[3]

United is not the only employee-owned airline in the United States. Tiny Kiwi International, which began flying with only two jets in September 1992, is 100 percent owned by its employees. Each pilot invests $50,000 in the airline and everyone else $5,000. Many of Kiwi's pilots are former Pan Am and Eastern pilots who lost their jobs when their former employers went belly-up. So highly motivated are Kiwi employees that flight attendants volunteer to clean cabins and pilots pick up trash under seats.[4] But employee ownership is not risk-free, as Kiwi's founder, Robert W. Iverson, learned the hard way. In February 1995, Iverson and his top lieutenants were ousted by Kiwi's employee-controlled board, which had developed a will of its own independent of its founder.

Avis: We Try Harder

That Avis, the number two automobile rental company in America, even survived its turbulent past is a minor miracle. Between the time it was founded in 1946 and the time it was purchased on behalf of its 11,500 U.S. employees in 1987 through an employee stock ownership plan, Avis had had eleven different owners, including ITT; Norton Simon; Esmark; and Kohlberg, Kravis, Roberts, to mention only a few.

The Avis Vision

*A*vis will be recognized as the preeminent company in the rent-a-car industry in the areas of:

• Customer service and satisfaction
• Employee participation
• Return to shareholders

Today Avis is thriving with 21,000 employees in 4,800 locations in 140 countries worldwide. To purchase Avis shares, an employee must work five years for the company. Seventy-one percent of Avis' shares are owned by employees and 27 percent by General Motors.

Avis' employees are empowered by employee participation groups (E.P.G.s) and task teams. E.P.G. representatives elected by their coworkers are charged with devising ways to improve service, enhance efficiency, and cut costs. They participate in monthly district-level meetings with managers to review operations and discuss ideas. The local groups also elect representatives to attend quarterly zone meetings, semiannual regional meetings, and an annual division-level meeting.

Through the local E.P.G. in Hawaii, Avis employees decided they wanted to dress in Hawaiian attire. As a result their outfits (using Avis' red-and-white colors) now include muumuus and Hawaiian tropical print shirts.

New York's E.P.G. initiated a "job swap" program in which employees in the local airports and the world headquarters swapped jobs for short periods to learn more about each other's work.

In 1994, task teams were formed to further intensify Avis' focus on customer service, to assess changing customer requirements, and to develop breakthrough services. Customer service task teams study customer input and emerging trends: the specialized needs of senior travelers, baby boomers, and more recently, the new generation of young adults called "Generation X."

Employee Ownership

My whole philosophy about business is that if you treat someone correctly and properly, chances are you'll get a good day's work out of them. . . . You have to keep emphasizing the importance of their roles, and you have to keep going out there to keep in touch with them.

JOSEPH VITTORIA
Chairperson and CEO, Avis

Avis' Chairperson and CEO, Joseph Vittoria, was a consultant to United Airlines as it evolved into an employee-owned company and now sits on its board of directors.

Steel Mills

In response to industry overcapacity, intense foreign competition, and pending financial disaster in the 1980s, more than a dozen steel mills in the United States averted extinction through worker buyouts. These included Republic Engineered Steel, Northwest Steel and Wire, McLouth Steel, and Weirton Steel—by far the largest and best known of the group. In return for wage and benefit reductions as well as work-rule concessions, employees, often with the help of the U.S. Steel Workers of America, negotiated the right to own these companies either in whole or in part.

When it became clear in 1982 that National Steel was going to let its Weirton Steel Division in West Virginia die on the vine, the Weirton Steel Corporation was formed to purchase the assets of the financially strapped division of National Steel. On January 11, 1984, the newly created company acquired the eighty-five-year-old integrated steel producer through an E.S.O.P.

Weirton Steel

*M*y father, his father, my son, four uncles, three brothers-in-law—even my mother during the war years—all of us worked here. So we go back some. We have roots in this mill.

JOHN BACKEL
Weirton steelworker

On March 7, 1989, the men and women of Weirton Steel made a commitment to make their facility a world-class steel mill by voting to decrease their own profit sharing and, instead, invest millions of dollars in capital improvements. Since then, more than $500 million has been spent to improve quality, increase yields, maximize productivity, and provide greater efficiency and better customer service. Through a combination of capital improvements and participatory management practices, Weirton has achieved many of its ambitious business objectives.

Smaller Enterprises

Four of the five employee-owned companies we have discussed have more than ten thousand employees. But the vast majority of the 2,500 or so employee-owned and controlled enterprises in the United States are much smaller, employing only a few hundred employees or fewer.

Lack of capital, inexperienced management, and unfriendly state laws are among the many obstacles to employee ownership. To help finance employee-owned businesses and other types of enterprises in impoverished areas of the country, a handful of so-called community development banks have appeared, the best known of which are the South Shore Bank of Chicago and the Self-Help Credit Union in Durham, North Carolina. In addition to employee-owned businesses, these nontraditional banks lend money to nonprofit groups, small rural businesses, microenterprises, and low-income home buyers.[5]

One of the most interesting examples of the widespread use of small employee-owned enterprises was in Hungary during the early 1980s. When the Hungarian Communist government began experimenting with capitalism and free markets, the only type of private businesses allowed were small employee-owned enterprises with no more than fifteen to twenty employees. To be an owner of a small business you had to be an employee. Nonemployee ownership was outlawed. This reflected a Marxist bias against nonworking-class control of private businesses. When a business began to grow and was faced with the twenty-employee limit, it would simply split into two separate businesses.

Cooperatives

Most of the employee-owned companies described thus far in this chapter are E.S.O.P.s rather than worker-owned cooperatives. Cooperatives have never been as popular in the United States as they are in Europe—particularly in Scandinavia. However, the Great Depression in the 1930s did create a small boom in rural electric cooperatives and rural telephone cooperatives, many of which have now been acquired by larger, private investor–owned utilities.

Of particular interest is a unique form of cooperative found in Israel known as the *kibbutz*. A kibbutz is an open-ended agricultural collective of several hundred members in which all property and production assets are owned by the cooperative. Membership is open to anyone and no initiation fee is required. Members are free to leave at any time. Land is leased from the Israeli government on a long-term basis. Wages and profits are shared equally by the members, and until recently there were no hired workers from outside the community. The kibbutz builds and furnishes houses for its members, pays for their medical care, provides their food and clothing, and even does their laundry. It also takes care of the elderly.

The kibbutzim have been strongly influenced by the emphasis placed on social justice and community by the biblical prophets. At least initially they were guided by the socialist ideal "from each according to his ability to each according to his needs." Each kibbutz is governed by a general assembly, which meets weekly and is open to all members. The general assembly elects officers and the secretariat, which coordinates the community. All resource allocation decisions are made by the community, including what is to be produced, when it is to be produced, how it is to be produced, and what is to be done with proceeds.

For the most part, the highly motivated kibbutzim are more efficient and more productive than other Israeli farms. Today most kibbutzim have diversified economies, which include manufacturing as well as farming.

In spite of the commitment of the kibbutzim to equality and democracy, women are sometimes treated as second-class citizens. Relatively few women are to be found in leadership positions in the kibbutzim. Most of them are employed in domestic services rather than in the more interesting and challenging jobs of the kibbutzim.

Kirkpatrick Sale has described the kibbutzim as "islands of collectivism in a capitalistic sea."[6] Although the kibbutzim have managed to avoid most of the social problems found in America, such as alienation, substance abuse, and crime, they have not escaped the negative effects of the ailing Israeli economy caused by the never-ending conflict between the Arabs and the Israelis. The combination of the unstable Israeli political scene and the sagging economy has caused the kibbutzim to back away from some of their socialist ideals. In recent years they have become more pragmatic, less democratic, and more profit-oriented. Kibbutzim can now form joint ventures with outside firms, have outsiders sit on their boards of directors, hire outside workers, and pay workers overtime. Notwithstanding some of these recent changes, the kibbutzim remain one of the purest forms of sustained democratic socialism in history.

By far the largest, most successful, and best-known work cooperatives in Europe—and perhaps the world—are the 170 worker-owned-and-operated cooperatives located in and around the town of Mondragon in the Basque region of Spain. From a small community-run training school started by a humble Catholic priest, José Maria Arizmendiarrietta, in wartorn Mondragon in 1943 evolved a $9 billion network of cooperatives creating more than 27,000 secure, well-paying jobs and serving more than 130,000 people. Among the enterprises in the Mondragon system are a large bank, a department store chain, appliance manufacturers, machine shops, high-tech firms, and technical assistance and research-and-development organizations.

Mondragon Principles

1. Open admission
2. Democratic organization
3. Sovereignty of labor
4. Instrumental and subordinate character of capital
5. Participatory management
6. Payment solidarity
7. Intercooperation
8. Social transformation
9. Universality
10. Education

The Mondragon cooperatives have survived the tyranny of Spanish dictator Francisco Franco, economic recessions, and intense competition. According to Roy Morrison in his highly informative book *We Build the Road As We Travel*, the Mondragon network has "forged innovative and responsive democratic decision-making structures, and invented increasingly sophisticated forms of democratic participation, cooperation, and community—an inspirational and practical model of democratic community economics."[7]

Public Ownership

Our story of employee ownership would be incomplete without reference to a special case of ownership in which a business is owned by the government—national, state (provincial), or local government. At least in theory, the enterprise is owned by *all* the people in the political unit, some of whom are employees.

Certainly the most extreme form of public ownership was the Stalinist model first introduced in the former Soviet Union in the 1930s and in Eastern Europe after World War II, which is only now being replaced by private ownership.

When Mikhail S. Gorbachev became the leader of the Soviet Union in 1985, the economic system he inherited was essentially the same system put in place by Joseph Stalin fifty years earlier. It was characterized by highly centralized state ownership, management, and control of the industrial, agricultural, and military resources of the country and was managed by a corrupt group of 250,000 self-perpetuating elites known as the *nomenklatura,* who had no incentive whatsoever to change the complex hierarchy of government and Communist Party organization.

Neither Soviet enterprise managers nor employees had much decision-making power. All important decisions were made in Moscow. Central planners decided what should be produced, how it should be produced, how it should be distributed, and what price should be charged. Decisions on wages, employment, training, safety, and local working conditions were also made in Moscow. Soviet workers were not encouraged to participate in any important decisions affecting the enterprise where they worked or their individual lives. Is it any wonder that Soviet workers were alienated?

An economic basket case, the former Soviet Union suffered from a plethora of well-known problems associated with the tightly controlled military state and rigid, highly centralized economic

system. These problems included economic stagnation, low productivity, shortages of food products and consumer goods, poor
morale on the part of managers and workers, and a serious gap
with the West in development of computers and other sophisticated technologies. These serious shortages of raw materials and
energy gave rise to production imbalances, unfulfilled production
quotas, the need for imports from the West, rising costs, and
foreign currency shortages. The huge Soviet military buildup during the 1970s and early 1980s pushed the country's scarce resources
to the limit.[8] The Soviet Union was also plagued with a number of
persistent social problems often associated with an authoritarian
closed society. These included corruption of government officials,
an extensive yet illegal black market for consumer goods and
services, social alienation of many of its people, high death rates
and infant mortality rates, and widespread alcohol abuse.

Perhaps the most unusual form of public ownership was the
Yugoslavian worker-managed economy. Its four distinguishing features included: (1) social ownership of capital, (2) employee self-
management, (3) market orientation, and (4) decentralization.

The Yugoslav model of socialism evolved out of the 1948 split
between Soviet leader Joseph Stalin and Yugoslav strongman Josip
Broz, known in the West as Tito. Enterprises were owned by society
as a whole and controlled by the employees. The government did
not have the right to tell a firm what to produce, how to produce
it, to whom it could sell its product, or how much it was allowed to
charge. The employees elected a workers' council—analogous to
an American board of directors—which hired a hierarchy of managers who actually ran the enterprise.

Yugoslav firms were highly market-oriented and decentralized
in much the same way as large American companies such as
General Motors and General Electric are. Individual businesses
were responsible for their own profitability.

Not unlike the Soviet economy and the economies of many
Western European nations, the Yugoslav economy performed rea-
sonably well during the 1950s and 1960s. However, during the
1970s and 1980s the rate of growth of output declined and inflation

soared. Although Tito died in 1980, Yugoslavia did not come completely unglued until 1991.

There were a number of fundamental problems with Yugoslavia's employee-managed enterprises. The government was the primary source of business development capital, and the process by which this capital was allocated to specific firms was highly political. To receive favorable treatment by the government authorities, an elaborate system of formal and informal payoffs evolved between firms and regulatory authorities.

Often the price of additional capital was adherence to restrictive governmental regulations. The elaborate set of regulations and arbitrary capital allocation decisions eventually took their toll on efficiency and inflation. Firms were rarely allowed to fail and go bankrupt in Yugoslavia. Even though employees received incentive bonuses linked to productivity and profitability, their behavior resembled that of workers in large American stockholder-owned companies. At one level, the hierarchical nature of Yugoslav companies was no different from their American "free enterprise" counterparts. At best, the Yugoslav employee-managed economy proved to be only a mixed success—not successful enough to overcome centuries of bitter internal political conflicts.

Private Versus Public Enterprise

The traditional political debate between the right and left revolves around the ownership of the means of production, to put it in Marxist terms: that is, around the question of whether business enterprises should be privately run or made public property. I would put it this way: the most important thing is that man should be the measure of all structures, including economic structures; the most important thing is not to lose sight of personal relationships—the relationships between man and his co-workers, between subordinates and their superiors, between man and his work, between this work and its consequences.

VACLAV HAVEL[9]

A popular myth perpetrated by conservative ideologues is that only privately owned profit-making enterprises are efficient and productive. People who work for inefficient, nonprofit enterprises including government are said to be the dregs of society. According to this distorted way of thinking, the only meaningful work that ever takes place is in the private sector. All nationalized companies are thought to be stodgy, bloated, and unimaginative. But this jaundiced view of the world overlooks that, outside of England, the former Soviet Union, and Eastern Europe, there are some very successful and very profitable state-owned companies. Some of the huge French state-owned companies are a case in point. Their mandate even under a socialist government was, "Become profitable or else." Their strategies differ little from their counterparts in the private sector.

Throughout the United States there are hundreds of small municipally owned gas, electric, water, and transportation utilities. Even though these are publicly owned businesses, the way of thinking in these firms is so strongly influenced by the private sector that the behavior of their managers and employees differs little from privately owned businesses.

Limitations of Employee Ownership

If efficiency is the criterion by which we judge the performance of employee-owned companies, then Avis, Publix, and UPS deserve high marks. But if meaningfulness of one's work is the criterion, then employee-owned businesses do not appear to be all that different from companies not owned by their employees.

For some employees the possibility of buying shares in the company in which they work has almost no appeal whatsoever. They suspect that employee ownership is just another form of manipulation by authoritarian, control-oriented managers. Just because a company is owned by its employees does not mean that it will be managed in a participatory fashion. Other employees want neither the responsibility nor the risk of ownership.

Some companies have merely traded control by outside investors for control by a specific group within the company such as the pilots of United Airlines. Employee ownership has been embraced by some managers as a sophisticated form of union busting. Large employee-owned companies arc often as undemocratic as their investor-owned counterparts. At companies such as UPS in which less than 10 percent of the employees are owners, tension can evolve between the ownership class of employees and nonowners.

Thus separation, alienation, and despair are as likely to occur in employee-owned companies as in traditional companies. What seems to be more important than who owns the company's shares is whether or not there is a shared vision of the future among the company's employees and managers alike. For this reason, participatory management may prove to be a much more feasible strategy for creating meaning in the workplace than employee ownership.

Chapter 8

PARTICIPATORY MANAGEMENT

We live with political institutions that celebrate the rights of individuals to express themselves, to assemble, to pursue happiness and individual purposes, to pick their own political leaders. Yet when we enter the factory door or the lobby of the business cathedrals in our major cities, we leave our belief in democratic principles in the car. The halls and chambers of these buildings have flourished on a very different set of beliefs and rituals.

PETER BLOCK
STEWARDSHIP[1]

One of the reasons why American companies have so much trouble competing with Japanese and European companies is that our growth in productivity has not kept pace with theirs. This reflects, in part, the fact that Japanese and European firms employ management practices which are much more participatory than those used by American companies.

Graduate schools of business have done little to encourage American companies to become either more participatory or more communitarian. Although most MBA programs require a course in organizational behavior, organizational behavior is often a euphemism for "how to manipulate employees so they will do what we want them to do."

As we saw with the story of Mike the steelworker, many companies employ the same management practices today that worked so well for them in the 1950s. However, the typical American worker at that time was not very well educated, grew up in the Depression, and respected authoritarian management. Today's workers are much better educated, more mobile, and have only limited experience with unemployment or poverty. The top-down authoritarian management philosophy of the 1950s creates alienation, high employee turnover, absenteeism, and declining productivity in the 1990s.

Hierarchical Management

As we have noted, American corporations are no more democratic than either the hierarchical Roman Catholic Church or the former Communist Party in Moscow. While espousing a philosophy based on individualism, democracy, and freedom of choice, most American companies do everything possible to silence dissent and quell any form of behavior which differs significantly from the norm. CEOs are the high priests of the corporate faith and enforcers of sacred business dogmas. Conformity and compliance are the twin pillars on which Corporate America rests.

Unfortunately, authoritarian management philosophy is not restricted to profit-making enterprises in America. Many public sector and nonprofit organizations have equally repressive management practices.

A General Accounting Office study of the U.S. Postal Service found that the irascible behemoth suffers from a "dysfunctional organizational culture" and that "no clear framework or strategy exists for moving agreed-upon values and principles down to the first-line supervisors and employees working at processing plants and post offices." The study concluded that labor-management problems at the Postal Service "are long-standing and have multiple causes that are related to an autocratic management style, adversarial employee and union attitudes, and inappropriate and inadequate performance management systems." Given such a scathing indictment by the GAO, it's a wonder the Postal Service works as well as it does.

The Politics of Work

*I*n Athens, the people could really exercise their power only because they spent most of their time on politics, while slaves did all the work which still had to be done.

ALBERT CAMUS
Notebooks 1935–1942[2]

Yet a U.S. Labor Department Commission on the Future of Worker-Management Relations concluded that 40 to 50 million workers—nearly a third of the nation's workforce—yearn to participate more actively in workplace decisions affecting their lives but lack the opportunity to do so.

Until very recently, managers of authoritarian, hierarchical American companies have shown little interest in sharing power with employees. What is called for is not sweeping new laws to protect the rights of employees, but a paradigm shift in the thinking of management and labor alike. The key to improved industrial relations lies in increased participation of employees in decision making. We should take a serious look at employee participation programs in countries such as Austria, Germany, Japan, Finland, and Sweden: self-managed work teams, total quality management teams, shop-floor participation, health and safety committees, joint labor-management training programs, joint task forces, and employee representation on boards of directors.

Hard Work

There is no substitute for hard work.

THOMAS ALVA EDISON

The good news is that employee participation is growing, diffused across the American economy and workforce. As much as 20 percent of the total workforce is now involved in some form of workplace participation. At a handful of "high performance" companies—including AT&T, Federal Express, General Electric, Motorola, and Xerox—participatory management is operating successfully. The bad news is that there is still a lot of deep-seated resistance to employee participation in decision making by management and labor alike. The reaction of Max and Lucas to participatory management was, "What's the big deal?"

Alternative Paradigms

Win-Win

Historically, American management has been accustomed to imposing its ideas on company employees rather than drawing on the combined experience of managers and employees. However, there does appear to be an increasing awareness on the part of labor and management that adversarial labor-management relations don't pay. The only real winners from our confrontational labor-management practices are our foreign competitors. Neither unreasonable antilabor policies nor irresponsible labor demands for shorter hours, narrow job classifications, and artificial workload limits do much to strengthen America's competitive position in the international marketplace.

Unfortunately, labor-management conflicts are not the only area of corporate management where a kind of *zero-sum* management style pervades. In game theory, where the term originated, a zero-sum is a situation where one player's gain exactly equals the other player's loss. Such thinking is widespread in Corporate America.

Another example of this destructive behavior occurs in the relationship between corporate management and the management of individual operating companies or business units owned by a large company. In these cases conflict revolves around such issues as strategic planning, resource allocation, budgeting, and control. The control of strategic planning in an operating company, for instance, is an issue ripe with potential for conflict. Typically, the general manager of an operating company negotiates with corporate management for investment resources, the request for such resources being based on a set of goals, objectives, and strategies proposed by the operating company itself. The individual operating company seeks as large an investment as possible from the parent company for as little cost as possible in terms of expected return for the corporation.

Corporate management, on the other hand, wants to minimize its investment in operating companies and seeks a high return from each of its business units. Fierce conflicts are not uncommon between corporate managers and operating company managers, and a type of "we" versus "them" syndrome sometimes arises over the control of the division-planning process. Indeed, in such companies, there is almost open warfare between division management and corporate management.

Another form of divisiveness encouraged by many decentralized companies is competition among operating companies for markets. In some companies, the alleged efficiencies associated with decentralized management may be negated by back-stabbing, cut-throat competition among operating company managers.

Most firms are, ultimately, organized around a number of specific functional activities such as finance, accounting, manufacturing, sales, and marketing. Zero-sum attitudes also constitute a big problem for functional management. Even in the case of highly decentralized conglomerates like General Electric, individual operating companies are typically organized along functional lines. In some cases, functional managers provide resources in support of a single product, in others they support a portfolio of products. No matter how you slice it, functional managers play an extremely important role in most American companies. It is they who control the scarce resources necessary to produce the goods and services provided by the firm.

In all too many companies, however, functional managers lord over jealously guarded fiefdoms. They manage their functional activities as though they were running independent businesses rather than providing one of several critical resources necessary for the survival and profitability of the company as a whole. Indeed, overzealous corporate executives frequently encourage their functional managers in this feudal behavior. Executives who hold a distorted view of the applicability of the nineteenth-century competitive model to intracompany activities are the source of many a company's problems. One industry in which this form of zero-sum conflict is particularly extreme is the electric utility industry. Electric utility executives often manipulate their functional resources as if they were political territories rather than interdependent activities, the smooth operation of which requires a high degree of cooperation among functional managers.

Further examples of the zero-sum mind-set include the confrontational relationships many American companies have with their competitors as well as federal, state, and local governments. Don't managers, employees, government, and society as a whole pay a high emotional, spiritual, and economic price for this mutually destructive behavior? If American businesses want to create a more meaningful and a more productive work environment, isn't it high time to emulate Max and Lucas and replace their zero-sum attitude with a win-win approach to problem solving?

Stewardship

In one of the most important management books of the decade, *Stewardship,* Peter Block effectively makes the case for replacing management's obsession with control with a philosophy based on service. "Stewardship is the willingness to be accountable for the well-being of the larger organization by operating in service, rather than in control, of those around us." It is "accountability without control or compliance."[3] According to Block, "Stewardship requires putting information, resources, and power in the hands of those people closest to making a product, designing a product or service, and contacting a customer."[4]

Stewardship

Stewardship holds the possibility of shifting our expectations of people in power. Part of the meaning of stewardship is to hold in trust the well-being of some larger entity—our organization, our community, the earth itself. To hold something of value in trust calls for placing service ahead of control, to no longer expect leaders to be in charge and out in front.

PETER BLOCK
Stewardship[5]

Nonprofit hospitals are examples of organizations in which stewardship is extremely important but often difficult to achieve. Most nonprofit hospitals have dual command systems—administrative and medical. In a typical community hospital the administrative staff has little or no control over the medical staff, that is, the physicians. Although the administrative staff has the ultimate responsibility for the quality and cost of hospital care, the physicians are essentially free agents, *not* accountable to the hospital staff. Building stewardship relationships with a group of egocentric doctors is one of the toughest challenges of hospital administration.

Among the many benefits associated with stewardship, claims Block, are that it can:

1. put real meaning into the ideas of service and accountability
2. create a workplace where every member thinks and acts as an owner
3. reintegrate the managing of work with the doing of work—everyone does real work
4. replace self-interest, dependence, and control with service, responsibility, and partnership
5. raise the productive capacity of work units and economic success of organizations
6. find practical ways for democracy to thrive in the workplace
7. refocus staff groups to serve core workers and give choice to the line
8. overturn pay and performance appraisal practices that support a managerial class system.

Empowerment

Conspicuously absent from many American firms is a high degree of trust between employees and managers. Yet without two-way trust it is impossible to sustain high levels of productivity. But *empowerment* is the linchpin of trusting relationships in the workplace. Without empowerment there can be no trust. Employees who do not feel empowered by the organization will not adopt the goals, objectives, and values of the company. To feel empowered, the employees must believe that the managers respect and appreciate their contributions.

Empowerment

*E*mpowerment embodies the belief that the answer to the latest crisis lies within each of us and therefore we all buckle up for the adventure. Empowerment bets that people at our own level or below will know best how to organize to save a dollar, serve a customer, and get it right the first time. We know that a democracy is a political system designed not for efficiency, but as a hedge against the abuse of power.

Empowerment is our willingness to bring this value into the workplace. To claim our autonomy and commit ourselves to making the organization work well, with or without the sponsorship of those above us.

PETER BLOCK
Stewardship[6]

Empowerment involves the redistribution of privilege as well as political power. In Peter Block's words, "Holding on to privilege is an act of self-interest, the antithesis of service and stewardship. If we wish to send ownership and responsibility down to the people close to the work we are required to send along privilege as their companion."[7]

In the story of the playhouse, Max, Lucas, and Morfar have all been empowered. In contrast, Mike the steelworker possesses almost no power at all at USX.

Co-creation

In chapter 3, we spoke of creativity as an important example of being in the workplace. In *Corporate Renaissance* creativity in the workplace was defined as "that process through which we, by meeting challenges and solving problems, reach the insight that our capacity is larger than what we believed it to be."[8]

Although creativity is certainly not impossible in an authoritarian hierarchical environment, stewardship and empowerment encourage more people to participate in the creative processes of an enterprise.

Co-creation

*A*ccept that you and everyone else are creative beings. By behaving towards others creatively, you can continually participate in co-creating what never existed before. Each of us can choose to be empowered by taking responsibility for shaping a positive, creative present and future.

Commit to fully participate in life by connecting with people and circumstances exactly as they are and exactly as things happen, without judging or preconditioning your thinking about them. Connect with the present state of what is happening and with the unlimited possibilities that are unfolding—the becomingness.

GEORGE LAND AND BETH JARMAN
Break-Point and Beyond[9]

There can be little doubt that Morfar, Max, and Lucas were engaged in co-creativity when they built the playhouse. We also saw evidence of co-creativity at Avis, Publix Supermarkets, and Mondragon cooperatives. And Mr. Fraley and his piano students most assuredly demonstrate co-creativity.

Shared Vision

Several years ago one of us was a consultant to the senior management of McDonald's. Although McDonald's had no formal strategic plan and no corporate organization chart, there was absolutely no doubt in anyone's mind what business McDonald's was in at that time—the hamburger business. From the CEO to individual store managers out in the boondocks, there was undivided commitment to growth by increasing the number of stores. I have never seen the likes of McDonald's in terms of the intensity of the shared vision of management and employees.

With one exception, Federal Express is another example of a large, successful American company with a well-defined vision. As we well know, FedEx is in the small parcel delivery business. In the early 1980s when FedEx's senior management had a temporary memory lapse and ventured into "Zap Mail"—an ill-conceived precursor of the fax machine—the company lost millions of dollars.

Shared vision is not only an important determinant of the financial success of a business, but it may contribute more to the employees' sense of meaning than employee ownership of the business.

One of the risks associated with authoritarian, hierarchical management is that it may distort the employees' vision of the future of the organization. Senior management may have one vision of the future, but employees several layers below may have quite a different view of where the company is headed.

In the typical hierarchically organized company, the vision of the future is defined by senior management without consultation with those who are expected to make the vision a reality. But with well-educated, affluent employees like Mike the steelworker, this model of management is counterproductive. It is difficult to find meaning in one's work if one has no voice in the underlying vision on which it is based.

However, as we have noted, broad-based participation in formulating the company's vision can be risky business. Employees who have been invited to help shape the corporate vision may also expect to share in the power and control of the organization. That was the bitter pill Kiwi International Airlines founder Robert W. Iverson was forced to swallow.

If work is to be meaningful for employees, separating the vision, execution, accountability, and control makes little sense whatsoever. Shared vision leads to shared trust and shared accountability. A tightly controlled top-down vision breeds distrust, which in turn leads to separation, alienation, and meaninglessness.

Shared vision represents the heart and soul of participatory management. Without shared vision work has no meaning—another important lesson of the playhouse story.

Vision

*V*ision originates and emanates from a feeling. It is a manifestation of some longing: for a life with outer and inner harmony; for a fair society; for a company focused on development, quality and service instead of on profitability. In other words, a vision expresses an inner desire for something we wish to see realized. A vision is moving. It is in continuous development and growth. It has life.

ROLF ÖSTERBERG
Corporate Renaissance[10]

Employee Participation

In response to some of the problems of separation, alienation, and meaninglessness described in this chapter and previous ones, there is a move afoot in Corporate America to reinvent large complex organizations. The most widely publicized form of this type of reorganization is usually called "downsizing" or "restructuring."

AT&T, the fifth largest industrial company in the United States with annual sales of $75 billion and a workforce of 304,500, split into a $50 billion communications service company, a $20 billion communications hardware company, and an $8 billion computer systems company—the largest corporate breakup in history. This followed on the heels of its 1984 court-ordered divestiture of seven separate regional telephone companies. So large was AT&T that its annual revenues exceeded the gross national product of 127 of the 159 countries for which World Bank tracks GNP.

About the breakup of the corporate behemoth, AT&T chairperson Robert E. Allen had this to say: "The complexity of trying to manage these different businesses began to overwhelm the advantages of integration. AT&T has to separate into smaller and more focused businesses."

Long before the announcement of the AT&T breakup, hundreds of large American companies were splitting off divisions and cutting the size of their workforces. IBM and General Electric had already shed 200,000 jobs each. Sears Roebuck and AT&T itself had previously eliminated more than 100,000 jobs before the AT&T breakup. A few months earlier ITT had announced that it was splitting up into insurance, industrial products, and resorts and recreation. Sears spun off Allstate insurance and its stock brokerage business, Dean Witter. General Motors unloaded EDS, its huge computer business.

Since the days of Henry Ford and Alfred P. Sloan, Jr., many Americans have subscribed to the view that not only are big companies good for consumers, good for employees, and good for investors, but that they do little damage to the environment. Former GM CEO Charles E. Wilson said it all: "What's good for General Motors is good for our country."

The recent spate of megamergers notwithstanding, the breakup of AT&T suggests there is an increasing realization among some that bigger may no longer be better. What is called the "law of increasing returns to scale," which misled us into believing that average costs would decrease with increases in company size, turns out to be a myth. If output continues to grow for a firm, there is some point beyond which additional increments of production result in reduced efficiency, higher costs, and lower profits. The firm may become virtually unmanageable. As the size of the firm increases, problems of alienation, motivation, coordination, communication, and control become more acute. The combined effect of increased global competition and decreasing returns to scale has forced hundreds of large corporations to restructure themselves.

The newly restructured corporations are leaner, meaner (more competitive), flatter, and more participatory than their predecessors. One way in which hundreds of American companies are going about reinventing themselves is through the use of self-directed teams. A team is a small group of people usually from different functional areas possessing complementary skills organized to solve a particular problem or achieve a specific objective. Among the companies making extensive use of self-directed work teams are Boeing, Caterpillar, Cunning Engine, Ford, IBM, 3M, and Tektronix. The rationale underlying the use of teams has been succinctly summarized by Jon R. Katzenbach and Douglas K. Smith in their book *The Wisdom of Teams:*

> In any situation requiring the real-time combination of multiple skills, experiences, and judgments, a team inevitably gets better results than a collection of individuals operating within confined job roles and responsibilities. Teams are more flexible than larger organizational groupings because they can be more quickly assembled, deployed, refocused, and disbanded, usually in ways that enhance rather than disrupt more permanent structures and processes. Teams are more productive than groups that have no clear performance objectives because their members are committed to deliver tangible performance results. Teams and performance are an unbeatable combination.[11]

Clearly, the Swedish playhouse project is a small-scale example of a self-directed team. Many high-tech companies employ the same

---

Reinventing Organizations

The opportunity for people to have lives that are rich with meaning, to reinvent the organizations that are the building blocks of society, and for both individuals and organizations to live according to a new worldview lies within our immediate grasp.

GEORGE LAND AND BETH JARMAN
Break-Point and Beyond[12]

---

concepts of team-building discovered by Morfar and his grandsons in the design of sophisticated computer hardware and software.

One particularly sophisticated application of teams to organizational problems is called *matrix management*.[13] Most hierarchical organizations are characterized by a one person–one boss chain of command. However, in a matrix organization, a multiple-command approach to management exists in which there are two or more lines of authority. Although often considered to be a quite radical approach to management, critics of matrix management fail to recognize that most families, as well as the government of the United States, are examples of multiple-command systems. Children in two-parent households are responsible to two authorities—the mother and the father—and so, coming up with solutions to family problems involving children usually requires negotiations between the child and the two parents. Similarly, the separation of the executive, judicial, and legislative branches of the United States government is a tripartite system of authority. This system of checks and balances is an integral part of our form of government and is a system that most Americans consider beneficial and necessary for preserving the rights outlined in our Constitution.

Beyond Hierarchies

I believe it is possible to run a company without hierarchies. Why shouldn't it be possible to have companies in which everyone is responsible, and equally so? Why should such companies be beyond our conceptual capacities?

ROLF ÖSTERBERG
Corporate Renaissance [14]

Aerospace and high-technology firms were among the earliest to employ matrix management. More than forty years ago, they became cognizant of the need to give equal attention both to project management and to the management of the technical resources required to support these projects. Competitive pressures, combined with rapidly accelerating technological change, necessitated that these firms come up with a balanced view of the management of projects that draw upon common resources. A typical aerospace firm—Boeing, for example—routinely has a number of big projects going all the time. As was becoming more and more apparent to these firms back in the 1950s, there were obvious efficiencies to be gained from encouraging project managers to share their engineers and scientists as well as their sophisticated equipment. Because of the nature of the aerospace industry, decisions concerning project management and critical resource management must often be made simultaneously rather than sequentially. Tradeoffs have to be made when project managers run up against resource constraints. Thus, the duality of projects and critical resources became increasingly apparent to industry executives as they responded to pressures both from the outside and from within their own organizations. Under these circumstances, a dual-command system made eminent sense.

Networks

Networks are people talking to each other, sharing ideas, information, and resources. The point is often made that networking is a verb, not a noun. The important part is not the network, the finished product, but the process of getting there—the communication that creates the linkage between people and clusters of people.

Networks exist to foster self-help, to exchange information, to change society, to improve productivity and work life, and to share resources. They are structured to transmit information in a way that is quicker, more high touch, and more energy-efficient than the other process we know.

JOHN NAISBITT
Megatrends[15]

Another reason that motivated such companies as Lockheed, Rockwell, TRW, Control Data, and Intel to turn to matrix management was a simple case of information overload. Increased uncertainty concerning the external environment, complicated by an increased organizational complexity—which had been caused by the simultaneous diversification of products and markets—led to an increased need both to receive and generate information. Traditional hierarchical organizations found it increasingly difficult to respond to these information processing requirements. Stated in other words, the interest in matrix management is merely a special case of society's need to replace hierarchical organizations with *networks*.

Although very few American companies have any employee representation whatsoever on their board of directors, such representation is required by law in most European countries. According to so-called *codetermination* laws in Germany and other European countries, firms with more than two thousand employees must have equal representation on their boards from employees and stockholders alike. If, for example, the board has twelve members, then six must be chosen by the employees and six by the stockholders.

Also mandated by law in Europe are enterprise councils, which give labor a voice in shop-floor policies such as wages, length of working day, firings, and layoffs.

The New Learning

*I*n the new learning—which tells us that every human being is not only unique, but also is a part of every other human being—the barriers which separate us collapse. There is no competition among human beings. There is no fear of not being successful, no fear of losing. In the new learning, there is no need for power and no room for hierarchical systems. The new learning and hierarchical systems are simply not compatible.

ROLF ÖSTERBERG
Corporate Renaissance[16]

Old Soldiers Never Die

In his farewell address to Congress in 1951, General Douglas MacArthur said, "Old soldiers never die; they just fade away," a description apropos of the slow death of hierarchical management practices in this country as well. No doubt inertia, resistance to change, and the newness of participatory management have all contributed to the snail's pace with which the new organizational learning has been accepted in the United States. But the real obstacle to the acceptance of participatory management is *power sharing*.

The risk of power sharing is loss of control on the part of traditional authoritarian managers—a higher price than most are willing to pay. Power sharing represents a clean break with a culture obsessed with owning, possessing, and controlling. Participatory management is a form of being rather than having.

In addition, participatory management is much more difficult to implement than authoritarian management. If you can get by with it, it's much easier to order an employee to do something than to try to reach a consensus with a group of well-educated, strong-willed employees, each with his or her own opinion about how something should be done. Team building, matrix management, and multiple-command administration are sophisticated management tools requiring substantially greater skill than hierarchical management.

More will be said about participatory management, power sharing, and the new learning in management in chapter 10, "Reinventing Work."

Chapter 9

VALUE-BASED MANAGEMENT

I finally realized that there was more to my business—to any business—than the numbers. There was its soul.

TOM CHAPPELL
THE SOUL OF A BUSINESS

In our quest for meaningful employment, if we are not in the position to do our own thing, we may at least want to pursue a career with an organization possessing values, ethical principles, and a sense of social responsibility consistent with our own. There are an increasing number of business firms which profess—and indeed practice—socially responsible values. Companies such as Ben & Jerry's, The Body Shop, and Tom's of Maine have a high degree of environmental integrity, engage in participatory management practices, and maintain a high level of social consciousness—and in some cases social activism.

Ben & Jerry's

With its avowed policy of "caring capitalism," Ben & Jerry's, the Vermont ice-cream maker, stands at the forefront of enlightened, socially responsible American businesses. Few companies are likely to replicate the phenomenal financial success of Ben & Jerry's— started by two guys from New York who learned how to make ice cream in a renovated gas station in 1978 with the help of a $5 correspondence course and an old-fashioned rock salt ice-cream-maker. Trading heavily on left-wing political, social, and environmental themes and its funky ice-cream flavors, Ben & Jerry's annual sales now exceed $150 million. Cherry Garcia, Chocolate Chip Cookie Dough, Rainforest Crunch, Chunky Monkey, and Wavy Gravy became household words.

New Age Management

In the ideal New Age company, employees are self-directed yet inspired by a visionary leader. The transformed workplace of the 1990s includes a flat organization chart, social responsibility, and good, clean entrepreneurial fun. It feels like a family or a friendly village, where everyone has flexible schedules to accommodate their personal lives. Managers encourage employees to do community work on office time, and everyone creates products that they themselves love.

They assure a cynical business world that companies can serve the common good and still make a profit. And they steadfastly assert that you can build an almost utopian community of workers at the same time that each individual employee reaches his or her developmental peak.

MARTHA NICHOLS
Harvard Business Review[1]

Before Ben Cohen stepped down as CEO, no senior executive at Ben & Jerry's had ever earned more than seven times the compensation of the lowest-paid worker with at least one year at the company. Its "partnershops" located in low-income areas are joint ventures with nonprofit, community-minded organizations aimed at creating employment opportunities, helping revitalize poor neighborhoods, and empowering neighborhood residents. In 1991, when dairy prices plummeted, Ben & Jerry's paid Vermont farmers premium prices for dairy products, reflecting what the company called its determination to support family farmers. The firm led the way in promoting a federal ban on the treatment of dairy cows with a genetically cloned growth hormone, bovine somatotropin.

Value-Based Management

*A*s long as we operate within [the] old paradigm, we are separated from our heart and values and feel powerless. We cannot suspend our values during the workday and think we will have them back when we get home. We're all interconnected. There is a spiritual dimension to business just as to individuals.

BEN COHEN
Ben & Jerry's

The company contributes 7.5 percent of its pre-tax earnings to the Ben & Jerry's Foundation, which makes contributions to charitable organizations that promote "creative social problem solving." Among the charities supported by the Foundation are the Children's Defense Fund and "1% for Peace," a nonprofit, nonpartisan organization devoted to improved global communication and understanding and cooperative multinational citizen initiatives. 1% for Peace supports congressional legislation which would allocate 1 percent of the defense budget to projects promoting peace. The company named its stick-pop ice-cream novelty product the "Peace Pop," and the packaging for the product contains literature describing 1% for Peace.

Ben & Jerry's purchases ingredients from suppliers that use their resources for progressive change: rainforest preservation, peace, employing the underprivileged, support for Native American businesses. Messages on millions of Ben & Jerry's ice-cream containers at various times have encouraged positive action on behalf of children's basic needs, world peace, rainforest preservation, family farms, and protesting the use of bovine growth hormone with dairy cows.

Ben & Jerry's has one of the most liberal employee benefit programs in the United States. Some of its many fringe benefits are: a company-matching pension fund; an employee stock purchase program; profit sharing; group life insurance; company-paid

---

Ben & Jerry's Mission

*B*en & Jerry's is dedicated to the creation and demonstration of a new corporate concept of linked prosperity. Our mission consists of three interrelated parts:

Product Mission—To make, distribute, and sell the finest quality, all-natural ice cream and related products in a wide variety of innovative flavors made from Vermont dairy products.

Social Mission—To operate the company in a way that actively recognizes the central role that business plays in the structure of society by initiating innovative ways to improve the quality of life of a broad community—local, national, and international.

Economic Mission—To operate the company on a sound financial basis of profitable growth, increasing value for our shareholders, and creating career opportunities and financial rewards for our employees.

---

medical and dental insurance; disability insurance; company-paid maternity, paternity, and adoption leave; adoption support; bank loan guarantees; tuition aid; on-site childcare; free ice cream; and free chocolate-chip cookies.

In 1993, when Ben & Jerry's informed its sole supplier of chocolate chip cookie dough, Rhino Foods, that it would not need any more cookie dough for at least three months, Rhino's employees came up with an uncommon solution to a common problem—overstaffing. Rather than laying off the surplus employees, Rhino's entered into an innovative employee exchange program with nearby Ben & Jerry's and Gardener's Supply of Burlington, a national mail-order company with a temporary influx of catalog orders.

The exchange program lasted for six weeks at Gardener's and for about two months at Ben & Jerry's. The host companies paid the salaries of guest employees, and Rhino's covered their fringe benefits. When Rhino's flow of orders returned to normal, the employees reclaimed their old jobs.

The Body Shop

"How do you ennoble the spirit when you are selling something as inconsequential as a cosmetic cream?"[2] In 1976, when Anita Roddick opened a small shop in Brighton, England, she sold 25 natural skin and hair products. Her original idea was disarmingly simple: Purchase cosmetics made from natural ingredients, in small containers. Today 420 nature-based cosmetics, skin, and hair-care products are sold by the Body Shop International in more than 1,200 shops in forty-eight different countries with product labels in nineteen languages. Annual sales top $500 million.

The Beauty Business

I hate the beauty business. It is a monster industry selling unattainable dreams. It lies. It cheats. It exploits women. Its major product lines are packaging garbage.

In my view the cosmetic industry should be promoting health and well-being: instead it hypes an outdated notion of glamour and sells false hopes and fantasy.

What is even worse is that the industry seems to have absolutely no sense of social responsibility.

ANITA RODDICK
Body and Soul[3]

Anita Roddick and her husband, Gordon, have attempted to make the Body Shop a model of social responsibility. The Body Shop encourages social responsibility by having its employees participate in community projects at home and abroad and getting involved in such activities as working in an orphanage for Albanian and Romanian children and helping to create a home in Albania for children with special needs. Other examples of social action supported by the Body Shop include projects to save the whales, to end testing of cosmetics on animals, and to help the homeless help themselves. Among the fundamental principles on which the Body Shop claims to operate are minimal packaging, close-to-source ingredients, and respect for people and the environment. The Body Shop's Trade Not Aid policy uses buying power to help direct money into the pockets of primary producers in Developing World countries such as Nicaragua, Mexico, Brazil, the Solomon Islands, and more recently, Siberia. According to Anita Roddick, the Trade Not Aid program is based on the following six principles:

1. respect for all cultures, religions, and environments
2. utilization of traditional skills and materials
3. trade lines that are sustainable as well as successful
4. use of replenishable natural materials
5. small-scale projects that can be easily duplicated
6. long-term commitment to all projects

The Human Spirit

I see business as a Renaissance concept, where the human spirit comes into play. It does not have to be drudgery; it does not have to be the science of making money. It can be something that people genuinely feel good about, but only if it remains a human enterprise.

ANITA RODDICK[4]

In her book *Body and Soul*, Ms. Roddick pitches her philosophy that "you don't have to lose your soul to succeed in business." Then she effectively articulates her vision of the Body Shop as "a force for social change, a powerful environmental lobby, and as a radical organization with an important contribution to make to both the business community and the developing world."[5]

Tom's of Maine

Founded in 1970 by Tom and Kate Chappell, Tom's of Maine is the country's leading producer of natural personal-care products including: toothpaste for adults and children, deodorant, antiperspirant, mouthwash, shampoo, and shaving cream. Although much smaller than either Ben & Jerry's or the Body Shop, Tom's of Maine is built upon its founders' vision of "a company managed both for profit and the common good of the community, the environment, and one another." The company takes pride in the fact that its products are made "using only pure, simple ingredients nature provides, and are packaged in ways which respect nature." The company donates at least 10 percent of its profits to charitable projects each year. Special emphasis is given to ethically motivated and environmentally sustainable economic development projects, as well as projects that benefit Native Americans and other indigenous peoples.

In the late 1980s, in response to a midlife existentialist crisis, Tom Chappell began taking courses at the Harvard Divinity School. While studying the works of theologian H. Richard Niebuhr and philosophers Martin Buber and Jonathan Edwards, Chappell came to believe that "common values, a shared sense of purpose, can turn a company into a community where daily work takes on a deeper meaning and satisfaction."[6]

Tom's of Maine

STATEMENT OF BELIEFS

• We believe that both human beings and nature have inherent worth and deserve our respect.
• We believe in products that are safe, effective, and made of natural ingredients.
• We believe that our company and our products are unique and worthwhile, and that we can sustain these genuine qualities with an ongoing commitment to innovation and creativity.
• We believe that we have a responsibility to cultivate the best relationships possible with our co-workers, customers, owners, agents, suppliers and our community.

• We believe that different people bring different gifts and perspectives to the team and that a strong team is founded on a variety of gifts.

• We believe in providing employees with a safe and fulfilling work environment, and an opportunity to grow and learn.

• We believe that competence is an essential means of sustaining our values in a competitive marketplace.

• We believe our company can be financially successful while behaving in a socially responsible and environmentally sensitive manner.

MISSION

• To serve our customers by providing safe, effective, innovative, natural products of high quality.

• To build a relationship with our customers that extends beyond product usage to include full and honest dialogue, responsiveness to feedback, and the exchange of information about products and issues.

• To respect, value and serve not only our customers, but also our co-workers, owners, agents, suppliers, and our community; to be concerned about and contribute to their well-being, and to operate with integrity so as to be deserving of their trust.

• To provide meaningful work, fair compensation, and a safe, healthy work environment that encourages openness, creativity, self-discipline, and growth.

• To contribute to and affirm a high level of commitment, skill, and effectiveness in the work community.

• To recognize, encourage, and seek a diversity of gifts and perspectives in our worklife.

• To acknowledge the value of each person's contribution to our goals, and to foster teamwork in our tasks.

• To be distinctive in products and policies which honor and sustain our natural world.

• To address community concerns, in Maine and around the globe, by devoting a portion of our time, talents, and resources to the environment, human needs, the arts, and education.

• To work together to contribute to the long-term value and sustainability of our company.

• To be a profitable and successful company, while acting in a socially and environmentally responsible manner.

Vermont

"The hills are still alive with the sound of town and village, of neighborhood, corner, and place."[7] Driving through Vermont, one is struck not only with the majestic beauty of the Green Mountains, the classic red barns and the covered bridges, but also with the picturesque patchwork pattern of small farms, villages, little rivers, ridges, hollows, and dirt roads, and the fact that there are no billboards. Because they like it that way, Vermonters have the highest percentage of unpaved roads in the country. Roadside billboards were banned in 1968.

From these initial impressions one suspects that Vermont may be different from other states—very different. Thriving in this peaceful bucolic environment are dozens of small, entrepreneurial-driven, socially responsible firms led by Ben & Jerry's. Without exception these high-performance companies trade heavily on Vermont's uniqueness—its tiny size, its rural nature, its tradition of freedom and democracy, and its strong sense of community.

Even though the Green Mountains pale in comparison with the Swiss Alps, Vermont business strategies have clearly been influenced by a number of common values shared with the Swiss, including independence, self-reliance, hard work, perseverance, and as previously noted a strong sense of community.

When IBM, Digital Equipment, Simmonds Precision, and St. Johnsbury Trucking began laying off hundreds of employees in the 1990s in response to a soft economy and corporate "restructuring," the knee-jerk reaction of Vermont's governor, economic development officials, chambers of commerce, and utility executives was a clarion call for action. But what they proposed to save Vermont jobs and attract industry differed little from strategies employed by low-wage states such as Arkansas, Mississippi, and North Carolina.

Green Mountain Strategies

1. Entrepreneurial-driven
2. Niche market
3. Premium quality
4. High value added
5. Upscale pricing
6. Community-based
7. Participatory management
8. Socially aware
9. Environmentally responsible
10. Vermont-oriented

The industrial future of Vermont lies not with corporate giants such as IBM, General Electric, and Lockheed Martin, but with small, homegrown entrepreneurial-driven companies such as Ben & Jerry's, Autumn Harp, Otter Creek Brewing, and Vermont Teddy Bear. To be sure few Vermont companies are likely to replicate the phenomenal success of Ben & Jerry's.

Small niche-market Vermont businesses such as Green Mountain Coffee, Rhino Foods, Danforth Pewterers, Vermont Bread, and Catamount Brewing produce high-quality, high-value-added products which sell for premium prices. Not unlike Switzerland's, the label "made in Vermont" has become synonymous with quality. Consider Vermont free-range turkeys, which sell for twice the price of ordinary turkeys—and are worth every cent of it. Other Vermont agricultural products with upscale prices include organic vegetables, flavorful (not plastic-like) tomatoes, drug-free beef, maple syrup, and a wide variety of specialty foods such as pasta, bread, and salsa. Vermont is the home of fourteen different salsa firms. Just as oil companies discovered they could increase their profits in the 1960s by going into the petrochemical business, so too did Vermont's Cabot Creamery find that its profits could be increased by the further processing of milk into cheeses, butter, yogurt, and other dairy products.

The Vermont Department of Agriculture has found that the word "Vermont" on a product's label yields 10 percent greater sales than might otherwise be the case. A product given the so-called Vermont Seal of Quality will on average experience yet an additional 10 percent sales increase. No one trades more heavily on the Vermont image and sells it more effectively than Ben & Jerry's.

Many small Vermont companies have a high degree of environmental integrity, engage in participatory management practices, and maintain a high level of social consciousness. Some of them you would not mind having in your own backyard. More than three hundred Vermont businesses belong to an organization called Vermont Businesses for Social Responsibility, whose mission is: To foster a business ethic in Vermont that recognizes the opportunity and the responsibility of the business community to set high standards for protecting the natural, human, and economic environments of our citizens.

Not surprisingly, Vermont's industries have one of the best track records in the nation in preventing the release of toxic chemicals to the air and water.

Consistent with Vermont's rural nature is the fact that it is a cityless state. However, the automobile, interstate highways, shopping malls, fast-food restaurants, suburban sprawl, state government centralization, and the union (consolidated) high school movement have taken their toll on Vermont towns and villages. Quaint villages that were once charming, such as Essex Junction, Richmond, Shelburne, and Hinesburg, are now little more than Burlington bedroom communities filled with apartments and condominiums. Others such as Grafton, Stowe, and Woodstock have been overrun by tourists—particularly skiers.

But in spite of these setbacks, community is still very much alive in many of the towns and villages of Vermont—in places like Bristol, Chelsea, Newport, Peacham, and Quechee to mention only a few. Although we have no prescriptive formula for a successful Vermont community, there are some elements common to many Vermont villages—a town hall, a school, a library, a community church, a post office, a country inn or a couple of bed-and-breakfast establishments, and several stores including a general store. The tradi-tional Vermont general store was an early precursor to the shop-ping mall. In the not too distant past, it was not uncommon for a general store to include a grocery store, an apothecary, a post office, a pub, a barbershop, and a doctor's office.

In June of 1993, the National Trust for Historic Preservation designated the entire state of Vermont as one of America's eleven most "endangered historical places." It was the first time a state had ever been placed on the list. That Vermont, of all states, would end up on the endangered species list took many people by surprise. A new $50 million shopping mall in Rutland and Wal-Mart's plans to open stores in St. Albans and Williston contributed to Vermont's being placed on such an inauspicious list. Vermont was the last state to succumb to the Arkansas mega-chain. Because some Vermonters consider Wal-Mart to be the enemy of small towns and small businesses, they fought its entry into the Green Mountain State tooth and nail. Montpelier is the only state capital in America without a McDonald's restaurant.

Suburban sprawl has turned the ten-mile stretch of Route 7 south of Burlington into the most unsightly ten miles of highway in the entire state. What was once a scenic drive near Lake Cham-plain to the quaint village of Shelburne has become a grotesque strip of fast-food restaurants, automobile dealerships, discount stores, and shopping malls. During most of the day there is bumper-to-bumper traffic between Burlington and Shelburne.

By 1970 real estate development had already produced such adverse effects in Vermont that the legislature passed an unprece-dented law aimed at controlling the abuse of Vermont's natural heritage—Act 250. According to Act 250, any substantial public or private real estate development project must obtain a permit certi-fying that the project will not adversely affect air and water quality, water supplies, roads and transportation, public schools, municipal services, scenic beauty, historic sites, wildlife, and irreplaceable natural areas.

Vermont's long-run economic future rests on three interde-pendent industries—tourism, agribusiness, and high technology.

Tourism is the state's flagship industry; it defines Vermont's external image, helps create demand for its agribusiness products, and entices high-tech entrepreneurs to the state. With nearly eight million tourists coming to Vermont each year, who spend $1.5 billion annually, tourism is a particularly effective way to sell Vermont to "flatlanders" (those not born in Vermont). Red barns, Holstein cows, maple syrup, and quaint New England villages are to Vermont what Brown Swiss cows, Emmentaler cheese, chocolates, and Alpine villages are to Switzerland.

One example of the link between farming and tourism is the increased popularity of farm tours and farm vacations. Vermont farmers have been surprised to find that urban families will pay them for the opportunity to spend a week working on the farm.

The presence of IBM, a state-of-the-art telecommunications switching network, and a well-educated workforce contribute to an environment conducive to high-tech entrepreneurial activity in microprocessors, computer software, information processing, robotics, avionics, and high-tech equipment. Burlington has attracted a large number of computer programmers, design engineers, word processors, and high-tech consultants who operate out of their homes.

Not everyone who is fed up with the crime, drug abuse, traffic, urban sprawl, and deteriorating quality of life in Urban America can pack up and move to Vermont. But Vermont does provide an alternative model to the dehumanized, mass-production, mass-consumption lifestyle which pervades our nation—a model which some states and some businesses may find appealing. In Vermont small firms work in harmony rather than in conflict with the local environment—a kinder, gentler approach to economic development than the "bigger is better" urban industrial paradigm. Business and government consciously cooperate to preserve a strong sense of community. Although Vermont may be too small to save our nation from the debilitating effects of separation, alienation, and meaninglessness, it does offer a communitarian substitute for the isolation, loneliness, and excessive individualism so prevalent in America. We can all learn from Vermont's experience.

The Dark Side

Many of these so-called socially responsible companies look a lot better from a distance than they do under more careful scrutiny. Attracted by the strong financial performance of Ben & Jerry's during the 1989–1992 period as well as the social responsibility hype generated by its founder and public relations genius, Ben Cohen, one of us was seduced into buying a few shares of Ben & Jerry's stock in 1993 for $32 a share. From Richmond, Virginia, where I was living at the time, it appeared that Ben & Jerry's could do no wrong. But sales began to level off in 1993 followed by a precipitous drop in earnings in 1994. The price of the stock had plunged to $12 a share when I lost heart and sold out.

Perhaps the financial reversal of Ben & Jerry's can be attributed to growing pains—the company had simply outgrown its two entrepreneurial founders, Ben Cohen and Jerry Greenfield. But an increasing number of questions were being raised by the press as to whether or not the management practices at Ben & Jerry's were consistent with the company's external image as a model corporate citizen.

For example, a nearby scoop shop in Shelburne, Vermont, successfully sued Ben & Jerry's for breach of a sales territory exclusivity agreement. There have also been allegations that the practices used by Ben & Jerry's to obtain retail shelf space differ little from those of its principal competitor, Häagen-Dazs ice cream—practices which in the 1980s Ben & Jerry's claimed were unfair. There is a dotted line separating some of the nonprofit charities created and supported by Ben & Jerry's and the company's normal marketing practices. Where does one draw the line between honest, socially responsible business practices and flagrant marketing manipulation? The book by former Ben & Jerry's CEO Fred Lager, entitled *Ben & Jerry's: The Inside Scoop,* suggests that the management style of the Vermont dream company is not nearly so participatory as its founders would have us believe.

When the founder of a value-based company feels obligated to tell us repeatedly how socially responsible his or her firm is, doesn't this kind of make you wonder what's really going on? Should one's morality be worn on one's sleeve? Do some of these firms go too far?

Journalist Jon Entine took Anita Roddick to task in an article entitled "Shattered Image: Is The Body Shop Too Good to Be True?" which appeared in the September-October issue of *Business Ethics* in 1994. Entine alleged that the Body Shop's claims of producing natural products are exaggerated and misleading, that the firm has serious quality-control problems, that its charitable contributions and progressive environmental standards fall short of the company's claims, and that the company has a history of making legal threats against journalists who question its pristine image. The Body Shop denied the allegations claiming that the article was "recycled rubbish" filled with "lies, distortions, and gross inaccuracies."

In a completely different vein, Martha Nichols had this to say about Anita Roddick in the *Harvard Business Review:*

> Anita Roddick would agree that the 1980s were morally bankrupt; yet she doesn't make the connection between the greedy grab for personal power and the New Age quest for self-fulfillment. Roddick and others express an unshakable faith in personal change because the myth of self-actualization remains seductive. Everyone likes to think they're in control of their own fate and that they can rely on their "gut" to make the right decisions.
>
> But much as New Agers want to believe in the power of personal transformation and creativity, entrepreneurs like Roddick often confuse themselves—their goals, political beliefs, dreams, and considerable talents—with the companies they create and the people who work for them. This confusion leads to both false humility and misleading assumptions about how their work translates to business as a whole.[8]

Throughout the 1980s, the upscale Portland, Oregon, mail-order house Hanna Andersson cultivated an image of caring and social responsibility. Yet when business turned down in 1993, it precipitously fired twenty employees—10 percent of its direct-labor force—without any warning whatsoever.[9] A surefire way to test the commitment of socially responsible businesses is to see how they behave when the going gets rough financially.

No More Catalogs

If you persist, you may succeed in having your name removed from some national advertising mailing lists and mail-order catalog lists, by writing to: Mail Preference Service, Direct Marketing Association, 11 West 42nd Street, P.O. Box 9008, Farmingdale, NY 11735.

And finally, lovable, cuddly, Vermont Teddy Bear Company was found to be in violation of the U.S. Fair Labor Standards Act and forced to pay sixty-six employees $62,400 in unpaid overtime pay. Not even teddy bears can be trusted nowadays.

——————— *Chapter 10* ———————

REINVENTING WORK

Work is a process through which we acquire experiences and insights and grow inwardly. The production of goods and services and economic return for work, are by-products of this process.

ROLF ÖSTERBERG
CORPORATE RENAISSANCE [1]

The Playhouse Revisited

Upon reflecting on my summer with Max and Lucas, I realize that it was a time of sharing, not just thoughts, but above all emotions. Along with all the joy there were also moments of sadness, anger, and frustration. There was much laughter, but also a few tears. But the love we shared was always present. There were moments when I had to work hard at letting go of my perfectionism, on my tendency to take on the CEO-role, and on my "adultism." I had to let go of wanting to plan and organize, and learn just to follow the flow of events created primarily by these two wonderfully flexible and sometimes unpredictable young human beings. All three of us learned some hard lessons about patience and the importance of expressing feelings while respecting the feelings of others. It was difficult for me to resist ordering the boys back a couple of times when they, frustrated with their "morfar," just left the scene. The entire experience for me was one of inner growth, and I was happy that I had ignored the advice of a neighbor who, after observing our labors and having his low regard for my practical skills confirmed, suggested that I buy a prefabricated house. Clearly, the playhouse itself had served as both a vehicle for and as a by-product of the real work: our personal growth and development as individuals and as members of a team.

These feelings confirmed that our summer activities had indeed been meaningful work. Work must be meaningful in order to be fulfilling. Meaningless work drains us of energy and transforms normal people into the "living dead," those who are physiologically alive, but spiritually, emotionally, and intellectually dead. Meaningful work, on the other hand, provides us with energy, fills our hearts with joy, and makes us feel alive.

In order to make work meaningful, it must be an integral part of life, not just that part of the day when we leave our "real" life to make the money we need to support what we refer to as spare time, that is, time when we are "spared" from work. Life like time is an integrated whole. It is not meant to be segmented into work time, spare time, and sleep time. There is no such thing as spare time, there is only life, and it is impossible to separate our work from our life.

In *Corporate Renaissance* in response to the aphorism "The measure of a man's work is not what he has obtained from it, but what he has become of it," I added:

> In these words lies the existential core of the new thought [about work]. We do not exist to survive, but to live. We do not exist to obtain things—to make money, to gain position and power, to collect possessions and thereby prove our worth to ourselves and others; we exist to learn, to develop and grow as human beings.
>
> The meaning of life is life itself—the process of living—and not what we accumulate along the way.[2]

To express this another way: Life is a process through which we, by meeting challenges and facing problems, collectively and individually, grow as human beings. Life is one continuous learning process, the purpose of which is growth. It is the internal process that is primary; all the external results are secondary.

Work is an important part of this learning process. The primary purpose of work is not to produce goods and services in exchange for paychecks but to serve as a vehicle (one among many others) for the real work we are here to do, to grow as human beings. Further, only work that is in harmony with what we deeply understand as our life purpose is meaningful.

Simple though the Swedish playhouse story may be, it also contains *all* of the important elements of a real-world workplace community—shared vision, common values, boundaries, empowerment, responsibility sharing, spiritual growth, tension reduction, education, feedback, and most important of all—friendship. And without even thinking about it, the three of us managed to emulate each of the strategies for meaningful work described respectively in the previous four chapters—self-employment, employee ownership, participatory management, and value-based management.

Did we invent a new kind of work on Vätö Island? Or did we simply rediscover the kind of work described here in chapter 2—work as a divine gift, a calling, a vocation? Certainly one subtle message from the playhouse is that child-rearing—at least in America—is a significantly undervalued form of work. Those who have the primary responsibility for the care and training of our children, whether in the home, the day-care facility, or the school, are not fully appreciated by our society and, therefore, are grossly underpaid.

Mike the Steelworker

Let us return to Mike the steelworker, introduced in chapter 3. As you may recall, Mike does not love his work at all. In fact, he behaves as if he hates it. He does not want more work; he wants less. Since his work provides no personal meaning, he becomes more and more alienated from his work, his family, society, and ultimately himself. It is obvious that his work disheartens him. It might finally kill him, either by the way he copes—drug and alcohol abuse—or by the stress of continuously—day after day, year after year—being forced or forcing himself to do something he heartily dislikes.

In chapter 3 we also spoke of Mike's grandfather. For four decades he performed the same boring, repetitive, and even hazardous work and had no problem working under the military-style management. This man was content with his lot. Why is it that today these same working conditions produce feelings of alienation, detachment, and complete disaffection in the grandson? Is there something wrong with Mike? Is there something wrong with the millions of workers in the industrialized world who, regardless of the work they perform and their positions within the corporate structure, are feeling the same emptiness and disaffection? Is there something wrong with the employees on the shopfloors, in the offices, or in the executive suites who feel the tightening in their stomachs and shortness of breath when they awaken from sleep, thinking of the workday before them?

No, there is nothing wrong with Mike or with any other disaffected, alienated worker. Nor is the reason for the divergent attitudes of Mike and his grandfather toward the same work environment to be found in the differences in their respective affluence, military experiences, and formal educations. It goes far deeper than that: Mike's core beliefs—what he deeply believes to be meaningful within—differ fundamentally from the beliefs held by his grandfather. To Mike's grandfather, life was a struggle for survival, a story about "making it" as well as he possibly could. Mike, on the other hand, has a completely different view of life and its meaning. Even though not conscious of it, Mike has embraced the same perception of life and the role of work as a learning and development process expressed by the story of the playhouse. Contrary to his grandfather, whose focus was externally directed and whose life purpose was defined by U.S. Steel, Mike's focus is directed toward inner growth, and he resents any external authority which attempts to define his life's purpose. In fact, his beliefs and perceptions are very similar to those of my grandsons, Max and Lucas. The difference between Mike and the two young Swedish boys is that the boys feel secure and have not yet discovered any conflicts between their belief system and the society in which they live, whereas Mike is experiencing exactly the opposite. He does not feel secure, cannot find a foothold, does not feel "at home" within himself, and is becoming more and more alienated from the world around him.

A Paradigm Shift

I believe that the differences in the life-views of Mike the steelworker and his grandfather stem from a paradigm shift in human thinking about which I wrote in *Corporate Renaissance* and shall now summarize.

We human beings, as a species, are experiencing a fundamental change of consciousness as a result of a common mental, emotional, and spiritual expansion. We are at the end of one evolutionary era, entering into a new one. This tremendous change is more profound and more revolutionary than most can imagine. We are experiencing a complete turnaround in our way of thinking.

We are abandoning an old, mechanistic perception of the world, of life, and of human beings and evolving toward a new view based on wholeness. We are abandoning a conceptual framework which gave extreme preponderance to the logical aspects of ourselves, ignoring our emotions, and adopting one which recognizes the importance of balancing thought and emotion. We are leaving an era where we fragmented the whole into pieces and created distance between ourselves and our environment. We are entering an era where the interconnectedness of life is recognized, where every human—though unique—is seen as a part of humanity as a whole—of every other human, of everything that is.

We are leaving an era marked by intellectual judgment, analysis, and calculation and are entering a new state of mind which recognizes the value of intuition; we are beginning to trust ourselves instead of numbers and external authority figures. We are replacing goal-directed, materialistic, result-oriented thinking and its inevitable greed and shortsightedness with an emotion-based perception that recognizes resultant products as secondary to the process which created them.

We are leaving an old perception of life as a struggle for survival, a competition judged by economic outcome, and adopting the notion that we are here, not to achieve, but to learn and grow as humans. We are beginning to perceive life as one continuous learning process in which we all—regardless of who we are—jointly participate with one another. We are starting to realize that the potential for growth and expansion is to be found only within ourselves. Consequently, we no longer define "growth" as economic and external, but as internal and human.

New Age Ideals

$\mathcal{N}$ew Age ideals have become increasingly popular
among baby boomers and busters, who find their fu-
tures uncertain in the wake of layoffs and restructur-
ings. In the fingernail-biting realm of networked
organizations, the continual competitive push for faster
production now vies with employees' calls for flexible
work schedules and more meaningful lives. How you define yourself—both on and off the job—is up for grabs,
as companies become ever more decentralized, diverse,
and unstable.

Companies can't afford to ignore the current epidemic
of white-collar job angst. Young professionals feel personal control and security slipping from their grasp
every day, and they're naturally drawn to New Age dis-
cussions of creative work and supportive communities.

MARTHA NICHOLS
Harvard Business Review [3]

One important consequence of the continuing shift of thought
is a changed idea of the primary purpose of work. Work is no longer
universally regarded as a vehicle for making money and estab-
lishing a career. Instead work is beginning to be recognized as a
vehicle for our personal growth and development. Consequently,
more and more people are no longer satisfied with being used as
tools for achieving material goals set by others, nor are they satisfied
with work that only serves as a tool for their own material goals.
There is a growing awareness that work has no real meaning unless
it serves as a tool for the higher purpose of our own growth and
development.

To fully understand the ramifications and implications of the
transition being experienced by Mike the steelworker and millions
of others like him, we need to point out some important factors of
the transition itself. This paradigm shift is neither the result of any
organized political or religious movement, nor merely an intellec-

New Work

New Work represents the effort to redirect the use of technology so that it isn't used simply to speed up the work and in the process ruin the world—turning rivers into sewers and rain into acid.

The purpose of technology should be to reduce the oppressive, spirit-breaking, dementing power of work—to use machines to do the work that is boring and repetitive. Then human beings can do the creative, imaginative, uplifting work.

So New Work is simply the attempt to allow people, for at least some of their time, to do something they passionately want to do, something they deeply believe in.

FRITHJOF BERGMANN
In Context[4]

tual process; it is a result of self-sustaining and irresistible human evolution driven by subconscious, emotional forces. Deep within

The Inversion of Work

The major institutions now optimize the output of large tools for lifeless people. Their inversion implies institutions that would foster the use of individually accessible tools to support the meaningful and responsible deeds of fully awake people. Turning basic institutions upside down and inside out is what the adoption of a convivial mode of production would require. Such an inversion of society is beyond the managers of present institutions.

IVAN ILLICH
Tools for Conviviality[5]

us, we have started *feeling* that what we have hitherto believed meaningful, no longer is. We have started feeling that the beliefs upon which we have built our lives are no longer valid.

Inherent within the process which validates these feelings is a transition period between incipient emotional awareness and full incorporation into conscious thought. For many of us, this time of transition—this time gap—is problematic and frustrating, as our heads and hearts pull in opposite directions, our heads telling us that "all we learned in school" is right, and our hearts telling us: "No, it's not right any more. It's, rather, the other way around."

Though such a fundamental shift requires time to be completed, it is interesting and noteworthy that when the number of people going through this process reaches a certain threshold, it comes about very rapidly—almost as an (emotional) explosion—in society at large. Historically, not many people are required to achieve this critical mass, and when enough have completed the transition and have changed their worldview, these changes begin simultaneously to manifest themselves within all the rest of us.

It is important to keep in mind that the prevailing institutions of our current societies and the systems (work, for example) that serve them can only persist if the people participating in their operation find them meaningful and agree to continue. Their very existence is the result of our believing them to be meaningful.

> $\mathcal{N}$ever doubt that a small group of thoughtful, committed citizens can change the world. Indeed, it's the only thing that ever has.
>
> MARGARET MEAD

When this process of changing beliefs expands into the thought systems of a large majority of people at the same time, the societal changes may be very dramatic, quite sudden, and utterly unexpected. The most striking recent example of this phenomenon was the collapse of Communism in the former Soviet Union and its satellite countries. Almost in disbelief, we watched on television the fall of the Berlin Wall, as well as the fall of a monolithic political system representing nearly 300 million people, occurring more or less on a daily basis. Most of us experienced those events as sudden, unexpected, almost unbelievable. Though they seemed sudden, they were the result of a long evolutionary process that in time had reached a critical threshold.

A Comparison of Mike the Steelworker and the Two Swedish Boys

There is neither anything wrong with Mike the steelworker nor was there anything wrong with his grandfather. His grandfather was a child of his time, a time when life was believed to be a struggle for survival. The purpose of life, as he perceived it, was to achieve material success as best he could. To him, work was the only means to that end. If he saw any other meaning in work, it was *duty*. According to the beliefs of his generation, one *should* work, and it was through work that one achieved value as a human being. That work could be something *fun* was almost unimaginable. Mike's grandfather was happy to have a job, any job. He made a living, he fulfilled his duty and thereby achieved value as a human being. The working conditions were a part of it all, and he saw no reason to question them.

Mike the steelworker and many of the workers of his generation, however, have severe problems, not only with working conditions but also within themselves. Mike is in the transition state, where the changes in his belief system are still subconscious and have not yet emerged as conscious thought. He *feels* resentment and alienation toward his work; he *feels* resentment toward society, but he does not really understand why. Torn between what his head tells him and what his feelings tell him, he has lost his mental balance and probably feels as though he is walking in a quagmire. His way of coping with the anxiety of this transition period is withdrawal, alcohol, drugs, and promiscuity. Others might refrain from those expressions by overworking—becoming superworkers (and heroes!)—as a way of coping. But all these behaviors mainly serve to numb the internal realizations struggling to emerge.

Flexible Work Options

*F*lexible work alternatives may be the single most important factor in allowing us to create the lives we want for ourselves and our families. Longer work hours have robbed us of irreplaceable hours with our families, depleted the energy we need to be fully contributing members of our community, and drained away the time it takes to be fully informed citizens.

While some are running out of time from overwork, others are hurting financially and emotionally from lack of work. At least some flexible work options serve to spread existing jobs further, creating a model for a saner, more humane work system.

KIM BUSH
In Context[6]

In contrast to Mike the steelworker, my grandsons, Lucas and Max, have no problems at all. They were, I dare say, born with a new way of looking at things. Their lives hang together. They *know* that life is a wondrous learning adventure. Should anyone try to tell them that they exist to survive, not to live, that person would be met with two young and startled faces and would be told: "Hey, you don't understand anything." They would shrug their shoulders and go back to whatever they might be doing. They and all others of their generation will never even consider employment in the traditional workplaces of today. I need to add here that one of the hard lessons I learned working with my grandsons was just how deeply ingrained in me was the old way of thinking. I had to work hard just to give in to the flow of events instead of measuring, planning, and organizing. At sixty-one years of age and having spent some fifteen years on my own transition, I discovered how far behind my grandchildren I was in my own development.

The Challenge

The dilemma of our time is that we human beings have grown beyond the institutions of our societies. They no longer meet our criteria for being meaningful. Consequently, we in Western societies risk a situation similar to that of the former Soviet Union: a sudden and utterly unprepared-for collapse of our system, resulting in chaos and tremendous human suffering. It is easy to hear the ticking bomb. There may be only one way to avoid the inevitable explosion: in *time* to understand what is going on and to start adapting our institutions and systems to the new set of beliefs, that is, to creating an institutional environment in which the fully conscious human can thrive, create, and become.

Despite the urgency, however, the political establishments of our societies will no doubt see these changes as a threat and, fearing them, will work hard to prevent any change that might jeopardize their positions.[7] To take on the task of transforming whole societies in one step is, therefore, improbable if not impossible. It must be done in stages, and as we must start somewhere, it's hard to imagine a more promising place to begin than with the workplace. Work is common—and close—to most of us, and it is in the workplace that most of us first start feeling alienated from the old institutions and structures. There is no other area where the clash between the old and the new becomes more evident than when a "new" human with a new idea for the purpose of work encounters a traditional company with the old-fashioned view of business—production solely for profit and results. Because business is so dependent upon people, and, in addition, is not only the dominant institution of our society, but also the institution most able to respond quickly to changes, it is clear that no other institution has a greater potential to serve as an agent of change.

Reinventing Work

- Work with personal and human development as its primary purpose.
- Business with the primary purpose of serving human development.
- Companies serving the market instead of exploiting it.
- Companies without any hierarchy or concentrations of power.
- Companies that do not strive to amass wealth and build economic value, but instead use their excess means to give energy to the process of their employees' personal development.
- Companies owned solely by the employees.
- A business life that is no longer production-oriented, but, instead, focuses on giving nourishment to life.
- A business life that does not draw, drain, or consume, but that nourishes, enriches, and augments.

ROLF ÖSTERBERG
Corporate Renaissance[8]

Business of the Future

In order to fulfill its destiny as an agent of change, business itself has to change. And these changes should not be limited to just "Band-Aids," such as making workplaces more physically attractive, making job tasks more satisfying, reducing the number of hierarchical levels, or introducing different forms of worker participation such as workplace democracy. Such measures are, of course, laudable, but, in the larger perspective, hardly more than a reorganization of the status quo. A fundamental transformation is required.

In *Corporate Renaissance* I spoke of the "existential crisis of business." To come to terms with this crisis, business needs to conduct a self-examination along these lines: "Yes, it is true that the primary purpose of business up to now has been to produce profits. And that has been as it should be. But is it valid any more? Obviously, it is no longer compatible with the new way of thinking about the primary purpose of work, and there is a widening gap between corporate managers and those who actually do the work. To close this gap we must change our thinking and completely redefine the very purpose of business." To repeat what I said in *Corporate Renaissance* about the new learning:

> The primary purpose of a company is no longer to make profit. Instead, the primary purpose of a company is to serve as an arena or platform for the personal and human development of those working in the company. Companies must become process oriented instead of results oriented. The results are by-products of the process.[9]

In no way am I suggesting that a company should not be profitable. Of course, "new" companies must generate the necessary energy for survival. Rather the focus is shifted from profitability to human development—process-orientation rather than results-orientation.

Work of the Future

The work of the future will be friendly toward the environment and will accept the environment's friendliness toward us; it will be interdependent rather than competitive and bellicose toward other humans; it will not exaggerate individualism or jingoism, sectarianism, or nationalism but will have a planetary worldview about it; it will not be about controlling the environment; it will not fall into the fallacy of an infinitely expanding mode of thinking about a finite reality, namely the Earth and its gifts to us; it will not succumb to economic determinism; it will look for its values and its creativity beyond technology alone.

MATTHEW FOX
The Reinvention of Work[10]

In this context, we propose three necessary organizational characteristics for successful businesses of the future. Each is derived from the notion that everything is interconnected, that there are no distances or differentiations among employees.

First, there is the matter of the *size* of future workplaces. It is not possible to achieve a sense of being part of a whole or to feel a closeness to our coworkers, to our work assignments, or to the workplace itself unless the number of people in the workplace is quite small. A commonly held view is that a workplace employing more than two hundred people will have considerable difficulty serving its purpose.

Second, there is the question of the *openness* of the workplace. It is impossible to feel that one is a part of a workplace in which everyone working there is not fully informed about what is going on. The present system in which most employees are denied access to relevant workplace information should be abolished.

Third, there is the *hierarchical* nature of most workplaces. Not only must hierarchical organization structures be abandoned, but hierarchical thinking as well.

Third Sector Work

*W*ith both the marketplace and government playing a reduced role in the work lives of millions of Americans, the Third Sector, or non-profit community, becomes the last best hope for both restoring the work life of the country and creating a new politics of meaning that can move our society into a post-market era.

While historians are quick to credit the market and government sectors with America's greatness, the Third Sector has played an equally aggressive role in defining the American way of life.

JEREMY RIFKIN
Tikkun[11]

The purpose of hierarchical organizations is to maintain power and control through fear. They create distances between people by encouraging mistrust and competition and are devastating to human creativity. In the business of the future, we will entrust people rather than mistrusting them. In the business of the future we will finally recognize that we all have different roles to play, but that no one role is more important or more valuable than any other role.

The ramifications of the transcendence of business into the new way of thinking extend far beyond the arenas of business and work. The transformation of work and business is an important and obvious first step in preparation for a transformation of our societies as a whole. A change in the nature and purpose of business and work could facilitate this larger, inevitable transformation and allow it to come about less traumatically than would be the case if business (like the former Soviet Union) continues to ignore what is happening before its very eyes.

Chapter 11

FROM NUTS AND BOLTS
TO HEART AND SOUL

Never work just for money or for power. They won't save your soul or build a decent family or help you sleep at night.

MARIAN WRIGHT EDELMAN
THE MEASURE OF OUR SUCCESS[1]

Whether called to work by God, by economic necessity, by our search for meaning, or by our yearning for community, our quest has revealed four possible states of meaning in the workplace. First, our work may be utterly meaningless, leading either to despair or to an intensified search for meaning outside the workplace. Second, we may find ourselves separated from others, ourselves, and the ground of our being in our work, precipitating feelings of alienation and an unfulfilled need for community and human connectedness. Third, we may either be victims or perpetrators of a competitive work environment characterized by owning, possessing, manipulating, and controlling other people. Fourth, our work may involve participating, sharing, and collaborating with others to create something of intrinsic social value which does not do irreparable damage to our physical environment and leads to spiritual and intellectual growth as well as emotional stability.

Our search for meaning in the workplace combines a trip inward with a journey outward in pursuit of human connectedness. Finding meaning in our work may prove to be elusive, if life beyond the workplace has no meaning. Likewise, if we spend most of each day engaged in meaningless work, then finding meaning outside of work may be no easy task. An inability to integrate one's personal life with one's life at work may prove to be a source of considerable pain and anxiety. But for some, a meaningless job may actually enable them to conserve the necessary energy required to engage in truly meaningful activities outside the workplace.

We have considered and evaluated five strategic options for finding meaning in the workplace—self-employment, employee ownership, participatory management, value-based management, and reinventing work. Without exception each of these strategies is biased toward the being mode of the life matrix described in chapter 3.

As a further refinement of our analysis, let us view work through two additional filters—the *human condition* and a set of reality-based *work options*. Regardless of the state of meaning of our work—meaninglessness, separation, having, or being—as human beings we are motivated to work by economic necessity, boredom, our obsession with work itself, greed, our need to comply, and our pursuit of spiritual, intellectual, and emotional balance.

The Human Condition

Economic Necessity

The vast majority of people in our country and elsewhere work to support themselves and their families. Although economic necessity may not be the only reason they are working, it is usually the most important reason.

Unfortunately, with the downsizing of Corporate America, tens of millions of high-paying manufacturing jobs have been lost, and the new jobs being created by our lackluster economy are frequently low-paying service jobs with no benefits, such as those provided by fast-food establishments like McDonald's and Kentucky Fried Chicken. As evidence of this trend, average per capita income adjusted for inflation has remained essentially flat for years. Between 1985 and 1993 median wages adjusted for inflation actually fell by 2.6 percent. For men the real wage rate decreased by 4.6 percent over the same period. And in the 1990s, as was the case in the 1980s, the very rich continue to get richer at the expense of the poor, who become even poorer.

There has been a significant increase in the percentage of people who work full-time yet cannot lift their family out of poverty without outside assistance. This problem has become particularly

Our Malaise

No wonder we head for the shopping malls and theme parks: we are no longer a nation of people who can find deep pleasure and creativity and satisfaction in the work we do, the things we make. The kinds of jobs that are ascendant in America are the jobs we once assumed that only poor people from other countries would want to perform: clerks, sales and service workers, janitors, watchmen, policemen, firemen, waiters, waitresses, cooks, busboys, dishwashers, maids and porters. Jobs that guarantee little except low wages, high anxieties, no advancement and a steady loss of self-esteem.

RON POWERS

acute among workers possessing few skills. A number of social ills are adversely affected by this trend, including record rates of welfare dependence, out-of-wedlock birth, child poverty, child abuse, and general social disaffection.

Twenty years ago a family of four could easily be supported with the income of only one family member. Today it takes two incomes to make ends meet in most families. Even though both parents are working harder than ever, they feel they are hardly holding their ground financially. They haven't got a clue as to how they will send their kids to college or whether their children will be able to find middle-class jobs and keep them. It is becoming increasingly obvious that the American dream of "a better life for our kids" is just that—a dream.

But for many Americans the search for meaningful employment is the search for a job—any kind of job. The comparative advantage of a college degree in the marketplace has diminished significantly over the past twenty years. Many a college graduate is unemployed.

Boredom

Although economic survival motivates many to work, others work simply because they have nothing else to do. They work because life has no meaning for them. In the words of Erich Fromm, "Modern man does not know what to do with himself, how to spend his lifetime meaningfully, and he is driven to work to avoid an unbearable boredom."[2]

Although drawn to work as a means to allay our boredom, if our work turns out to be meaningless, we may become even more bored than before. Whether our work be that of an assembly-line worker, a traveling salesperson, or a mindless bureaucrat, our common enemy is boredom.

The Assembly Line

For the great majority of automobile workers, the only meaning of the job is in the paycheck, not in anything connected with the work or the product. Work appears as something unnatural, a disagreeable, meaningless and stultifying condition of the paycheck, devoid of dignity as well as of importance. No wonder this puts a premium on slovenly work, on slowdowns, and on other tricks to get the same paycheck with less work. No wonder that this results in an unhappy and discontented worker—because a paycheck is not enough to base one's self-respect on.

PETER F. DRUCKER
Concept of the Corporation[3]

Nothing better illustrates the separation, alienation, and boredom of meaningless work than the plight of traveling salesman Willy Loman in Arthur Miller's classic drama *Death of a Salesman*. After years of deluding himself and his family into believing that one day he will land "the big sale," Willy finally comes to realize that it is all a big lie—indeed his whole life is a lie. Unable to bear the pain of reality staring him in the face, Willy commits suicide.

Meaningless and Boring Work

$\mathcal{B}$ut there is far more serious and deep-seated reaction to the meaninglessness and boredom of work. It is a hostility toward work which is much less conscious than our craving for laziness and inactivity. Many a businessman feels himself the prisoner of his business and the commodities he sells; he has a feeling of fraudulence about his product and a secret contempt for it. He hates his customers, who force him to put up a show in order to sell. He hates his competitors because they are a threat; his employees as well as his superiors, because he is in a constant competitive fight with them. Most important of all, he hates himself, because he sees his life passing by, without making any sense beyond the monetary intoxication of success.

ERICH FROMM
The Sane Society[4]

Obsession

So meaningless are the lives of many that they literally bury themselves in their work. Their only escape from the pain of their unanswered existential questions is work. The only way they can cope with the agony of separation, meaninglessness, and eventually death is to maintain a feverish level of activity.

Why Work?

$\mathcal{D}$o we work to live? Or live to work? That is the question.

The Economist

Many who complain about how hard they work not only have more income than they will ever spend but enough material wealth to last a lifetime. Work is their obsession, and income is the primary measure of their success and social status. Without their work they would be nothing.

Obsessive Work

With the collapse of the medieval structure, and the beginning of the modern mode of production, the meaning and function of work changed fundamentally, especially in the Protestant countries. Man, being afraid of his newly won freedom, was obsessed by the need to subdue his doubts and fears by developing a feverish activity. The outcome of this activity, success or failure, decided his salvation, indicating whether he was among the saved or the lost souls. Work, instead of being an activity satisfying in itself and pleasurable, became a duty and an obsession.

ERICH FROMM
The Sane Society[5]

Paul Hawken has suggested in *The Ecology of Commerce* that the behavior of many corporate executives is remarkably similar to that of a drug addict. Addiction is a way to suppress our feelings. Work, television, video games, technology, sex, and sports can all be addictive if we rely on them to cope with our feelings of separation and meaninglessness.[6]

Having It All

No message is repeated more often by television, our political leaders, and our entire culture than "You can truly have it all." For men and women alike, "having it all" means working sixty hours a week, being a good mother or father, belonging to the Rotary Club, serving on the school board, being active in the local church or synagogue, owning a home, and jogging for an hour each day. But there is no way we can have it all. If we want to have a meaningful family relationship, we have to work less—not more. Alternatively, if our career is all that matters, then maybe we should forgo having a family. Life is full of choices and tradeoffs. Emotionally, spiritually, intellectually, and physiologically, having it all is an impossible dream.

Running Out of Time

Nothing in the modern workplace, and very little in society at large, encourages us to take our time, or be satisfied with what we have. We're being presented instead with a future where we will have to work harder, but have even less leisure time than we do today, if we are going to maintain our way of life. We are speeding up our lives and working harder in a futile attempt to buy the time to slow down and enjoy it.

PAUL HAWKEN
The Ecology of Commerce [7]

Compliance

One of the inherent risks of human resource management tools such as industrial psychology and organizational development is that they can quite easily be used to manipulate compliant employees. Although it is certainly possible to use self-managed teams, matrix management, and total quality management (TQM) as tools to help create a more meaningful workplace environment, they can just as easily become cynical tools of management manipulation.

Surprising though it may be, many well-educated, affluent employees such as Mike the steelworker, who resent authoritarian management practices, are still amazingly passive and compliant. They offer little resistance to manipulative management practices disguised as participatory management practices.

Human Engineering

. . . An attempt to treat the worker and employee like a machine which runs better when it is well oiled . . . the manipulation of the worker's psyche . . . if he works better when he is happy, then let us make him happy, secure, satisfied, or anything else, provided it raises his output and diminishes friction.

ERICH FROMM
The Sane Society[8]

Balance

Finally, we work to fulfill our spiritual, intellectual, emotional, and physiological needs. What E. F. Schumacher calls *Good Work* in his book bearing that title comes very close to what might be called *meaningful work.*

Good Work

First, to provide necessary and useful goods and services.

Second, to enable every one of us to use and thereby perfect our gifts like good stewards.

Third, to do so in service to, and in cooperation with, others, so as to liberate ourselves from inborn egocentricity.

E. F. SCHUMACHER
Good Work[9]

Work Options

Career Resilience

Until recently it was not uncommon for an individual to prepare himself or herself for a lifetime career in a particular job. Those who went to work for IBM, AT&T, General Motors, and Proctor and Gamble right out of college retired there forty or fifty years later. If one went to medical school, dental school, business school, or law school, it was with the full expectation that one would devote one's life to a career in one of these respective fields.

But the restructuring of Corporate America, about which we have spoken, has shattered the illusion of guaranteed lifetime employment with any corporation. Tens of millions of corporate employees have been forced out of their jobs into a hostile job market with which they are ill-prepared to deal. Overnight they have had to confront their obsolescence in a rapidly changing world.

Career-Resilient Workforce

. . . A group of employees who not only are dedicated to the idea of continuous learning but also stand ready to reinvent themselves to keep pace with change; who take responsibility for their own career management; and, last but not least, who are committed to the company's success. For each individual, this means staying knowledgeable about market trends and understanding the skills and behaviors the company will need down the road. It means being aware of one's own skills—of one's strengths and weaknesses—and having a plan for enhancing one's performance and long-term employability. It means having the willingness and ability to respond quickly and flexibly to changing business needs. And it means moving on when a win-win relationship is no longer possible.

Harvard Business Review[10]

Whether it be from career burnout, a midlife crisis, or existential anxiety, many people abruptly change their careers, switching to some wholly unrelated field after ten or twenty years in the same profession. Clearly, assembly-line jobs are not the only repetitive jobs that can lead to separation and alienation. Take the examples of the ophthalmologist or optometrist. Without the meaning derived from focusing on the patient as a human being, how many repetitive eye examinations is it possible to conduct without going crazy? Dentists are known to have quite a high suicide rate. And how long can one survive in a meaningless government bureaucracy—or any kind of bureaucracy, for that matter?

Career resilience and adaptability are the bywords of the 1990s. Whether self-imposed or externally imposed, career change has become an important element of economic survival. Young people need to give more thought to the likelihood they will experience multiple careers over their lifetime. Our public schools and colleges need to do a better job of preparing students for a life in which job changes are the rule not the exception. Trite though it may sound, putting all of one's eggs in one career basket is a very high-risk game educationally, economically, and psychologically.

The New Covenant

*U*nder the new covenant, employers give individuals the opportunity to develop greatly enhanced employability in exchange for better productivity and some degree of commitment to company purpose and community for as long as the employee works there. It is the employee's responsibility to manage his or her own career. It is the company's responsibility to provide employees with the tools, the open environment, and the opportunities for assessing and developing their skills. And it is the responsibility of managers at all levels to show that they care about their employees whether or not they stay with the company. The result is a group of self-reliant workers—or a *career-resilient workforce*—and a company that can thrive in an era in which the skills needed to remain competitive are changing at a dizzying pace.

Harvard Business Review [11]

The Leisure Alternative

Part of the lesson of Mike the steelworker is that well-educated, affluent, blue-collar workers and white-collar workers alike both want more leisure time rather than less. Yet according to Paul Hawken, during the past twenty years, "Our standard of living has not increased, real wages have not risen, and for the very first time since the Industrial Revolution, our work week is getting longer, not shorter."[12] In stark contrast to their counterparts in the United States, European companies such as Volkswagen shorten their workweek during economic downtrends to save jobs. Around the world, reformers are increasingly calling for a thirty-hour workweek.

About leisure time, Matthew Fox said,

We need to take up activities that truly engage us with ourselves and others—music, painting, poetry, dance, massage, cooking, hiking in nature—not to pursue prizes or with a mentality of judgment but rather as we would approach prayer itself, for that is what these actions are: acts of meditation and art as meditation.[13]

---

*A*ll work and no play makes Jack (Jill) a dull boy (girl).

JAMES HOWELL
Proverbs

Human Connectedness

Above all meaningful work is about human connectedness. For work to be meaningful it must enhance our ability to connect with others, ourselves, and the ground of our being—spiritually, intellectually, emotionally, and physiologically. Whether working alone or in a group, meaningful work leads to the growth and development of the individual worker as well as the group as a whole.

In the search for meaning in the workplace, it is impossible to overemphasize the physical dimension of work in terms of our connectedness to other workers or to the consumers and users of what we produce. The touching, sharing, cooperating, and physical participation which take place in the workplace are of critical importance to meaningful work. Can people working in a business survive without physical interaction with customers? How many writers can write without any direct contact with readers? For how long can musicians perform without an audience? Or artists without patrons?

For this reason we remain skeptical of claims of a community of isolated individuals working alone at their computer terminals in their homes connected to each other only through E-mail or the information highway. We believe there is no substitute for physical connectedness in the workplace.

Homeostasis

For spiritual quest, intellectual growth, emotional balance, and physiological stability to exist in the workplace, Paul Hawken has suggested that we need a combination of what he calls *sustainable businesses* and a *restorative economy*. Hawken defines a sustainable business as one which

1. Replaces nationally and internationally produced items with products created locally and regionally.
2. Takes responsibility for the effects it has on the natural world.
3. Does not require exotic sources of capital in order to develop and grow.
4. Engages in production processes that are human, worthy, dignified, and intrinsically satisfying.
5. Creates objects of durability and long-term utility whose ultimate use or disposition will not be harmful to future generations.

6. Changes consumers to customers through education.[14]

A restorative economy is

> a prosperous commercial culture that is so intelligently designed and constructed that it mimics nature at every step, a symbiosis of company and customer and ecology . . . redesigning our commercial systems so that they work for owners, employees, customers, and life on earth without requiring a complete transformation of humankind.

> A restorative economy will have as its hallmark a business community that coevolves with the natural and human communities it serves. This necessitates a high degree of cooperation, mutual support, and collaborative problem-solving. It depends on very different skill-sets than those that are being drummed into us in sports, movies, and business schools. Competition for the consumer or between businesses is impractical, wasteful, expensive and degrading to all involved.[15]

Soul Crafting

The search for meaningful work is no different from the search for meaning elsewhere. It involves a search for grounding—a sense of connectedness to ourselves, to our coworkers, to the environment, and to the ground of our being.

The bottom line of our quest is soul crafting—the care and nurturing of our soul. Both in the workplace and elsewhere our soul is the sum of our deeds, our work, our creations, our experience, our love, our joy, our pain, and our suffering. Our soul is continuously evolving throughout our entire life.

It was not entirely by chance that we began this book with the story of the playhouse. Embedded in this tale are most of the elements of meaningful work—the call to work, work as a vocation, and work as our real hobby. And as we have noted, not only is the playhouse venture a metaphor for meaningful work, it is also an example of an ideal workplace community.

Meaningful work is a form of *intentional activity freely given* by an individual who *decides,* possibly in collaboration with others, what is to be done, how to do it, when it is to be done, with whom to do it, and for whom the benefits are intended. Such work may or may not result in financial remuneration. Thus, one of life's greatest challenges is *finding affordable meaningful work.*

Not unlike the playhouse, which "had to have a key-hole and a key," meaningful work is an integral part of our soul in which resides the key to a happy death.

We not only possess the ability to bestow meaning on our work, but we have a responsibility to do so. Although we are free to choose the meaning of our work and life, the responsibility for crafting our soul is inescapable. How do we nurture our soul in the workplace? How do we fine-tune it? We do so through being—through our creations, through our workplace relationships, and by reinventing work.

The Mystery of Work

*T*he source of things is a deep, dark mystery. Being is indeed born out of nonbeing, surprise from doubt, light from darkness, joy from sorrow, hope from despair. Even the most everyday kinds of work can be seen as a joining together of space—nothingness—and our hands at work.

MATTHEW FOX
The Reinvention of Work [16]

Our soul embodies our personal philosophy—our sense of meaning, our values, our ethical principles, and our sense of social responsibility. It is the sum of our joys and sorrows, our hopes and fears, and our goals, objectives, and strategies both in the workplace as well as elsewhere. It reflects who we are and who we want to become. Our image of what we want our work to become resides deep within our soul.

The only thing we can count on when we die is that our soul—our very being—will survive on this earth through the work we have done, the creations we have left behind, the personal friendships we have experienced, the communities in which we have lived and worked, and the joy and sorrow to which we have given birth. That may very well be all there is to life and work, but that is a lot.

Gandhi on Soul Crafting

*T*here must be recognition of the existence of the soul apart from the body, and its permanent nature, and this recognition must amount to a living faith; and, in the last resort, nonviolence does not avail those who do not possess a living faith in the God of Love.

GANDHI

By assuming responsibility for the meaning of our work, we also take control of our destiny. It may not be a rosy picture, or at least not the picture we had in mind when we began our quest. The search for meaning in the workplace is not for the faint of heart.

Work As Grace

*O*ur work is meant to be a grace. It is a blessing and a gift, even a surprise and an act of unconditional love, toward the community—and not just the present community that may or may not compensate us for our work, but the community to come, the generations that follow our work.

MATTHEW FOX
The Reinvention of Work[17]

Baden Powell's Last Message

$\mathcal{D}$ear Scouts—

If you have ever seen the play *Peter Pan*, you will remember how the pirate chief was always making his dying speech because he was afraid that possibly when the time came for him to die he might not have time to get it off his chest. It is much the same with me, and so, although I am not at this moment dying, I shall be doing so one of these days and I want to send you a parting word of goodbye.

Remember, it is the last you will ever hear from me, so think it over.

I have had a most happy life and I want each of you to have as happy a life too.

I believe that God put us in this jolly world to be happy and enjoy life. Happiness doesn't come from being rich, nor merely from being successful in your career, nor by self-indulgence. One step towards happiness is to make yourself healthy and strong while you are a boy, so that you can be useful and so can enjoy life when you are a man.

Nature study will show you how full of beautiful and wonderful things God has made the world for you to enjoy. Be contented with what you have got and make the best of it. Look on the bright side of things instead of the gloomy one.

But the real way to get happiness is by giving out happiness to other people. Try and leave this world a little better than you found it, and when your turn comes to die, you can die happy in feeling that at any rate you have not wasted your time but have done your best.

"Be prepared" in this way, to live happy and to die happy—stick to your Scout promise always—even after you have ceased to be a boy—and God help you to do it.

Your friend,

BADEN POWELL OF GILWELL
Founder of the Boy Scouts

Work may either be meaningless, a contributor to separation and alienation, a form of having, or a source of being. Even though no cosmic source of the meaning of work has been revealed to us, we are drawn to the notion that the purpose of life is to die happy and that the only way to die happy is to learn how to *be* both in our work and in the rest of our life.

Soul-Destroying Work

*T*hat soul-destroying, meaningless, mechanical, monotonous, moronic work is an insult to human nature which must necessarily and inevitably produce either escapism or aggression, and that no amount of "bread and circuses" can compensate for the damage done—these are facts which are neither denied nor acknowledged but are met with an unbreakable conspiracy of silence—because to deny them would be too obviously absurd and to acknowledge them would condemn the central preoccupation of modern society as a crime against humanity.

E. F. SCHUMACHER
Small Is Beautiful[18]

To die happy we must first assume personal responsibility for the meaning of our life. Living means coming to terms with, rather than avoiding, pain and suffering in our life and in our work. To have a happy death we must confront meaninglessness and separation through being—resisting whenever possible the temptation merely to have. Being involves caring, loving, sharing, and participating in community with others in the workplace and elsewhere. If only we could be as lucky as Max and Lucas, and find our very own playhouse on which to work!

The crafting of our soul in the workplace requires a well-defined sense of direction, discipline, and commitment. Self-employment, participatory management, community, value-based management, employee ownership, and reinventing work can each be effective tools of soul crafting if properly used. The spiritual, intellectual, emotional, and physiological dimensions of our life demand continuous attention both in the workplace and otherwise. Is it possible to die happy, if we spend most of our life engaged in work that is utterly meaningless?

We must take leave of you now. We have to go to work!

Notes

Preface

1. Thomas H. Naylor, William H. Willimon, and Magdalena R. Naylor, *The Search for Meaning* (Nashville: Abingdon Press, 1994), p. 206.
2. Ibid., p. 11.
3. Rolf Österberg, *Corporate Renaissance* (Mill Valley, Calif.: Nataraj, 1993), pp. 12-13.

Chapter 1: THE SEARCH FOR MEANING

1. Ivan Illich, *Tools for Conviviality* (Berkeley, Calif.: Heyday Books, 1973), p. 11.
2. Ibid., p. 13.
3. I have written a book on the challenges of being a pastor and the potential for burnout. See William H. Willimon, *Clergy and Laity Burnout* (Nashville: Abingdon Press, 1989).

Chapter 2: OUR CALL TO WORK

1. See *The Works of Aristotle*, ed. E. D. Ross (Oxford: Oxford University Press, 1921), vol. 10, pp. 1337*b*, 1277*a*, 1277*b*. This classic disdain for work was carried over into the thought of most of the early Christian fathers. Bernard of Clairvaux, for instance, taught that the highest vocation was contemplation, the lowest was the life of the "world," meaning all secular employment. See George W. Forrell, "Work and the Christian Calling," *Lutheran Quarterly* (May 1956), pp. 105-18.

2. Quoted in David O. Moberg, "Christian Perspectives on Work and Leisure," in Carl F. Henry, ed., *Quest for Reality: Christianity and the Counter Culture* (Downers Grove, Ill.: Intervarsity Press, 1973), p. 122.

3. See my extended discussion of the "Fall" in William H. Willimon, *Sighing for Eden: Sin, Evil, and the Christian Faith* (Nashville: Abingdon Press, 1985), particularly chaps. 6 and 7.

4. See Abraham J. Heschel, *The Sabbath* (New York: Farrar, Straus & Giroux, 1975).

5. Benjamin Kline Hunnicutt, *Work Without End: Abandoning Shorter Hours for the Right to Work* (Philadelphia: Temple University Press, 1988), chaps. 1–3, tells the interesting story of the involvement of American rabbis in the struggle for shorter working hours in this country through the sabbath movement.

6. Jeremy Rifkin, "After Work," *Utne Reader* (May-June 1995), p. 60.

7. Jaroslav Pelikan, ed., *Luther's Works: Genesis, Chapters 1–5* (St. Louis: Concordia, 1958), vol. 1, p. 103. "It looks like a small thing when a maid cooks and cleans and does other housework. But because God's command is there, even such small work must be praised as a service of God far surpassing the holiness and asceticism of all monks and nuns," p. 100.

8. Marc Kolden, "Luther on Vocation," *Word and World,* vol. 3, no. 4, pp. 382-90.

9. Gustaf Wingren, *Luther on Vocation* (Philadelphia: Muhlenberg, 1957).

10. John Oliver Nelson reflects a Lutheran view when he says that "no matter how contented men and women may be in their daily existence, it is insignificant unless it is consciously related to worship of the true God." "Christian Vocation and Daily Work," *Social Action* (May 1956), pp. 7-15.

11. John Calvin, *Institutes,* ed. J. T. McNeill, Library of Christian Classics (London: Oxford University Press, 1960), p. 725.

12. See the discussion of Weber in Richard H. Tawney, *Religion and the Rise of Capitalism* (New York: Harcourt, Brace and Co., 1926); also, Trevor J. Wigney, "Reflections on the Protestant Work Ethic in Australia," *St. Mark's Review* (March 1979), pp. 2-10.

13. A number of years ago, pastoral psychologist Wayne E. Oates coined the term "workaholic" to speak of the religious roots of addiction to incessant work. See his *Confessions of a Workaholic* (Nashville/New York: Abingdon Press, 1971).

14. Peter Carnley, "A Theology of Vocation to Work," *St. Mark's Review* (March 1979), pp. 11-15.

15. Quoted by Robert G. Middleton, "Revising the Concept of Vocation for the Industrial Age," *The Christian Century* (October 29, 1986), p. 943.

16. United States Catholic Conference, Publication No. 825, Office of Publishing Services. The numbers cited are the paragraph numbers in the text. We are indebted to Stanley M. Hauerwas for much of our interpretation of *Laborem Exercens,* in chap. 7 of his *In Good Company* (Durham, N.C.: Duke University Press, 1995).

17. Louis T. Almen, "Vocation in a Post-Vocational Age," *Word and World,* vol. 4, no. 2, pp. 131-40.

18. Robert Linhart, *The Assembly Line* (Amherst: University of Massachusetts Press, 1981), p. 16.
19. Karl Barth, *Church Dogmatics* III/4 (Edinburgh: T. & T. Clark, 1961), p. 599.
20. Dorothy Sayers, *Creed or Chaos* (New York: Harcourt, Brace, 1949), pp. 54-55.
21. Donald W. Shriver, Jr., "Vocation and Work in an Era of Downsizing," *The Christian Century* (May 17, 1995), pp. 538-40.

Chapter 3: THE MEANING OF WORK

1. Charles Handy, *The Age of Paradox* (Boston: Harvard Business School, 1994), p. x.
2. Albert Camus, *The Myth of Sisyphus* (New York: Alfred A. Knopf, 1955), pp. 119, 121.
3. Larry Dossey, address to Mystics and Scientists Conference, Winchester, England, April 3, 1993. Quoted in Matthew Fox, *The Reinvention of Work* (San Francisco: HarperSan Francisco, 1994), p. 14.
4. Albert Camus, *Notebooks 1935–1942* (New York: Paragon, 1991), p. 85.
5. Erich Fromm, *The Art of Loving* (New York: Harper & Row, 1956), p. 88.
6. Karl Marx, *Economic and Philosophical Manuscripts* (London: Lawrence and Wishart, 1959), p. 138.
7. Camus, *Notebooks 1935–1942*, p. 85.
8. See William H. Willimon and Thomas H. Naylor, *The Abandoned Generation: The Crisis in American Higher Education* (Grand Rapids: Wm. B. Eerdmans Publishing Co., 1995).
9. Paul Hawken, *Ecology of Commerce* (San Francisco: HarperSan Francisco, 1993), p. 159.
10. Ivan Illich, *Deschooling Society* (New York: Harper & Row, 1970), dust jacket.
11. Kirkpatrick Sale, *Human Scale* (New York: Coward, McCann & Geoghegan, 1980), p. 352.
12. Peter Block, *Stewardship* (San Francisco: Berrett-Koehler, 1993), p. 45.
13. Graef A. Crystal, *In Search of Excess* (New York: W. W. Norton, 1991), pp. 27-28.
14. Viktor E. Frankl, *Man's Search for Meaning* (New York: Washington Square Press, 1984), p. 133.
15. George Land and Beth Jarman, *Break-Point and Beyond* (New York: Harper Business, 1992), p. 218.

Chapter 4: THE SEARCH FOR COMMUNITY IN THE WORKPLACE

1. Tom Chappell, *The Soul of a Business* (New York: Bantam, 1993), p. 60.
2. M. Scott Peck, *A World Waiting to Be Born* (New York: Bantam, 1993), p. 353.
3. Thomas J. Peters in Carolyn R. Shaffer and Kristin Anundsen, *Creating Community Anywhere* (New York: Jeremy P. Tarcher/Perigee, 1993), p. 113.

4. Charles Handy, *The Age of Paradox* (Boston: Harvard Business School, 1994), pp. 259-60.

5. Leopold Kohr, *The Breakdown of Nations* (New York: E. P. Dutton, 1978), p. 95.

6. Peter Block, *Stewardship* (San Francisco: Berrett-Koehler, 1993), p. 45.

7. Chappell, *Soul of a Business,* p. 63.

8. Peck, *A World Waiting,* p. 353.

9. Rolf Österberg, *Corporate Renaissance* (Mill Valley, Calif.: Nataraj, 1993), p. 31.

10. Shaffer and Anundsen, *Creating Community Anywhere,* p. 121.

Chapter 5: MANAGEMENT PHILOSOPHY

1. Paul Hawken, *The Ecology of Commerce* (New York: Harper Business, 1993), p. 1.

2. See Thomas H. Naylor, William H. Willimon, and Magdalena R. Naylor, *The Search for Meaning* (Nashville: Abingdon Press, 1994), pp. 169-76.

3. Before attempting to write a management philosophy, a manager may find it useful to have a look at chapter 6 of *The Search for Meaning,* which describes how to go about writing one's own personal history, personal philosophy, and personal strategic plan.

4. Margaret Kaeter, "Mission: Impossible?" *Business Ethics* (January-February 1995), p. 24.

5. Leopold Kohr, *The Breakdown of Nations* (New York: E. P. Dutton, 1978), p. xviii.

6. Kaeter, "Mission: Impossible?" p. 26.

7. Peter Block, *Stewardship* (San Francisco: Berrett-Koehler, 1993), p. 45.

8. Vincent Barry, *Moral Issues in Business* (Belmont, Calif.: Wadsworth, 1979).

9. Thomas M. Mulligan, "The Moral Mission of Business," in *Ethical Theory and Business,* ed. Tom L. Beauchamp and Normal E. Bowie (Englewood Cliffs, N.J.: Prentice-Hall, 1992), p. 66.

10. Laura L. Nash, "Ethics Without the Sermon," *Harvard Business Review* (November-December 1981), pp. 79-90.

11. Thomas H. Naylor, "The Trouble With Child-Sponsorship Charities," *The Chronicle of Philanthropy* (January 12, 1995).

12. Mulligan, "Moral Mission," p. 67.

13. Hawken, *Ecology of Commerce,* pp. 121-22.

14. Ibid., p. 54.

Chapter 6: SELF-EMPLOYMENT

1. Erich Fromm, *Escape from Freedom* (New York: Avon, 1965), p. 302.

2. E. F. Schumacher, *Small Is Beautiful* (New York: Harper & Row, 1973), p. 158.

3. Irvin D. Yalom, *When Nietzsche Wept* (New York: Basic Books, 1992), p. 188.

4. Charles Handy, *The Age of Paradox* (Boston: Harvard Business School Press, 1994), p. 76.
5. Kirkpatrick Sale, *Human Scale* (New York: Coward, McCann and Geoghegan, 1989), pp. 141-42.
6. Yalom, *When Nietzsche Wept,* p. 177.
7. According to an analysis by the *New York Times* ("The Downsizing of America," March 3, 1996, p. 27) of data compiled by the U. S. Labor Department, more than 43 million jobs were eliminated in the United States between 1979 and 1995. However, during this same period the number of nonagricultural jobs in the country increased from 90 million in 1979 to 117 million in 1995, despite the 43 million jobs lost over this span. But more often than not, those who lost a full-time job got a new one that paid less than the old.
8. C. W. Mills, *White Collar* (New York: Oxford University Press, 1951), p. 220.
9. Schumacher, *Small Is Beautiful,* pp. 215-16.
10. Ibid., pp. 119-20.
11. Frank Bryan and John McClaughry, *The Vermont Papers* (Post Mills, Vt.: Chelsea Green, 1989), p. 242.
12. Louis Uchitelle, "More Are Forced into the Ranks of Self-Employment at Low Pay," *New York Times,* November 15, 1993, p. 1.

Chapter 7: EMPLOYEE OWNERSHIP

1. Len Krimerman and Frank Lindenfeld, eds., *When Workers Decide* (Philadelphia: New Society Publishers, 1992), p. 2.
2. Ibid., pp. 3-5.
3. Adam Bryant, "After 7 Years, Employees Win United Airlines," *New York Times,* July 13, 1994, p. A1.
4. Adam Bryant, "One Big Happy Family No More," *New York Times,* March 22, 1995, p. D1.
5. Keith Sinzinger, "North Carolina's Self-Help Credit Union," *Washington Post,* April 25, 1993, p. A3.
6. Kirkpatrick Sale, *Human Scale* (New York: Coward, McCann & Geoghegan, 1989), p. 387.
7. Roy Morrison, *We Build the Road As We Travel* (Philadelphia: New Society Publishers, 1991), back cover page.
8. Thomas H. Naylor, *The Gorbachev Strategy* (Lexington, Mass.: Lexington Books, 1988), pp. 5-6.
9. Vaclav Havel, "Work, By Any Other Name," *Columbia* (Fall 1990), p. 40.

Chapter 8: PARTICIPATORY MANAGEMENT

1. Peter Block, *Stewardship* (San Francisco: Berrett-Koehler, 1993), p. xii.
2. Albert Camus, *Notebooks 1935–1942* (New York: Paragon, 1991), p. 207.

3. Block, *Stewardship*, p. xx.
4. Ibid., p. 33.
5. Ibid., p. 41.
6. Ibid., p. 9.
7. Ibid., p. 47.
8. Rolf Österberg, *Corporate Renaissance* (Mill Valley, Calif.: Nataraj Publishing, 1993), p. 44.
9. George Land and Beth Jarman, *Break-Point and Beyond* (New York: HarperCollins, 1992), pp. 215-16.
10. Österberg, *Corporate Renaissance*, pp. 77-78.
11. Jon R. Katzenbach and Douglas K. Smith, *The Wisdom of Teams* (New York: Harper Business, 1993), p. 15.
12. Land and Jarman, *Break-Point and Beyond*, p. 135.
13. For a more complete treatment of *matrix management*, see Thomas H. Naylor, *The Corporate Strategy Matrix* (New York: Basic Books, 1986).
14. Österberg, *Corporate Renaissance*, p. 51.
15. John Naisbitt, *Megatrends* (New York: Warner Books, 1982), pp. 192-93.
16. Österberg, *Corporate Renaissance*, p. 40.

Chapter 9: VALUE-BASED MANAGEMENT

1. Martha Nichols, "Does New Age Business Have a Message for Managers?" *Harvard Business Review* (March-April 1994), p. 52.
2. Anita Roddick, *Body and Soul* (New York: Crown Publishers, 1991), p. 22.
3. Ibid., p. 9.
4. Quoted by Nichols, "New Age Business," p. 56.
5. Roddick, *Body and Soul*, back cover.
6. Quoted by Nichols, "New Age Business," p. 53.
7. Frank Bryan and John McClaughry, *The Vermont Papers* (Post Mills, Vt.: Chelsea Green Publishing, 1989), p. 64.
8. Nichols, "New Age Business," p. 56.
9. "Too Good to Be True," *Inc.* (July 1994), pp. 34-43.

Chapter 10: REINVENTING WORK

1. Rolf Österberg, *Corporate Renaissance* (Mill Valley, Calif.: Nataraj, 1993), p. 95.
2. Ibid., p. 93.
3. Martha Nichols, "Does New Age Business Have a Message for Managers?" *Harvard Business Review* (March-April 1994), p. 4.
4. Frithjof Bergmann, interview by Sarah van Gelder, "New Work, New Culture," *In Context* (Winter 1993–1994), p. 54.
5. Ivan Illich, *Tools for Conviviality* (Berkeley, Calif.: Heyday Books, 1973), p. 116.
6. Kim Bush, "Flexible Work Options," *In Context* (Winter 1993–1994), p. 39.

7. Historically, similar fundamental shifts such as the Copernican revolution have precipitated extreme responses to protect existing institutions—decapitations, incarcerations, religious persecution, witch-hunts, and the Inquisition. It is to be hoped that changes in the workplace will encounter more subtle forms of resistance.
8. Österberg, *Corporate Renaissance,* p. 123.
9. Ibid., p. 33.
10. Matthew Fox, *The Reinvention of Work* (San Francisco: HarperSan Francisco, 1994), pp. 75-76.
11. Jeremy Rifkin, "The High-Tech Populism in the Information Age," *Tikkun* (May/June 1995), p. 47.

Chapter 11: FROM NUTS AND BOLTS TO HEART AND SOUL

1. Marian Wright Edelman, *The Measure of Our Success* (New York: Harper Perennial, 1993), p. 40.
2. Erich Fromm, *The Sane Society* (New York: Henry Holt, 1955), p. 179.
3. Peter F. Drucker, *Concept of the Corporation* (New York: John Day, 1946), p. 179.
4. Fromm, *Sane Society,* pp. 183-84.
5. Ibid., pp. 178-79.
6. Paul Hawken, *The Ecology of Commerce* (New York: Harper Business, 1993), pp. 123-24.
7. Ibid., p. 126.
8. Fromm, *Sane Society,* p. 182.
9. E. F. Schumacher, *Good Work* (London: Abacus, 1980), pp. 3, 4.
10. Robert H. Waterman, Jr., Judith A. Waterman, and Betsy A. Collard, "Toward a Career-Resilient Workforce," *Harvard Business Review* (July-August 1994), p. 88.
11. Ibid.
12. Hawken, *Ecology of Commerce,* p. 144.
13. Matthew Fox, *The Reinvention of Work* (San Francisco: HarperSan Francisco, 1994), p. 161.
14. Hawken, *Ecology of Commerce,* p. 144.
15. Ibid., pp. 15, 159.
16. Fox, *Reinvention of Work,* p. 51.
17. Ibid., p. 89.
18. E. F. Schumacher, *Small Is Beautiful* (New York: Harper and Row, 1973), p. 39.